BLING
THE HIP-HOP JEWELLERY BOOK

BLING
THE HIP-HOP JEWELLERY BOOK

REGGIE OSSÉ & GABRIEL A. TOLLIVER

BLOOMSBURY

First published in Great Britain in 2006

Copyright © 2006 by Reggie Ossé and Gabriel A. Tolliver

The moral right of the authors has been asserted

Bloomsbury Publishing Plc, 36 Soho Square, London W1D 3QY

A CIP catalogue record for this book is available from the British Library

ISBN 0 7475 7803 6
ISBN-13 9780747578031
10 9 8 7 6 5 4 3 2

Printed in Singapore by Tien Wah Press

All papers used by Bloomsbury Publishing are natural, recyclable products made
from wood grown in well-managed forests. The manufacturing processes conform
to the environmental regulations of the country of origin.

www.bloomsbury.com

THIS BOOK IS DEDICATED TO BROOKLYN,
THE HEART AND SOUL OF NEW YORK CITY,
AND OF COURSE TO EVERYONE EVER
INVOLVED IN HIP-HOP, PAST, PRESENT, AND
FUTURE. YOU CONTINUE TO INSPIRE AND ARE
THE SOUNDTRACK OF OUR LIVES.

Introduction

Bling is a concept, a sound effect, a light refraction, a lifestyle. Bling is status. Bling is loud. There's nothing as intoxicating as walking into a nightclub blinged with your best on your wrist, chest, ears, all eyes on you, captivated by your glow as you silently acknowledge your props. Mankind has been fascinated with bling since prehistoric days: Fossils dating back to 40,000 BC have been discovered with cavemen rocking gold bling. Where does our attraction to the shine of a dope-rope chain or the bling of a diamond-encrusted Rolex come from? With the proliferation and consistent success of hip-hop culture as an ever-growing way of life among people around the globe, we have observed, in the form of bling, the current permutation of man's love affair with all things shiny. From the corners of Nostrand Avenue and St. John's Place in Brooklyn to the fashion runways of Paris, it is all but impossible not to notice hip-hop's influence on the way we rock jewelry. The influences shaping today's form of bling can be attributed to the edgy-slick marriage of two factors: (1) the birth and rise of hip-hop in American culture and (2) the values pumped constantly into the psyche of a young hip-hop nation during the era of Reaganomics. From the late 1970s to the mid-1980s, Hollywood provided a quick fix for a generation left disappointed by the broken promises of the civil rights era. We were fed a high-calorie diet of materialism in movies like *Scarface* (the blueprint for gangster rap), and in TV shows like *Dallas* (who can forget O.G. J. R. Ewing?), *Dynasty* (kindergarten for the likes of Lil' Kim, Trina, and Foxy Brown), *Miami Vice* with its smooth criminals and fly-ass cops; and finally, the sperm that birthed current lifestyle shows like *MTV Cribs—Lifestyles of the Rich and Famous*.

The lesson that the hip-hop generation took from that period was that in order to be accepted in this society, one had to be successful. Not successful as defined by shows like the *Jeffersons* and the *Brady Bunch*, but mega-*paid*. *Big*, *large* and *in charge*! Back then, hip-hop was a fad (as we were constantly being told by our parents, older cousins, uncles, and anyone else in our community who doubted the hype). As this "fad" evolved and became a major cultural movement, the hip-hop generation began to dictate lifestyles that perfectly mirrored what was fed to it during its formative years by mainstream society. *Bling* has since become synonymous not just with jewelry (it was included in the 2000 *Oxford English Dictionary*) but with hip-hop culture in general since the mid-1990s. Bling is anything and everything today in pop culture that expresses wealth to the highest degree. And bling is here to stay.

one
BLING!

THE FIRST DISTINCT AND UNDOUBTED REFERENCE TO DIAMONDS
OCCURS IN ROMAN LITERATURE OF THE FIRST CENTURY. THE DIAMONDS
KNOWN TO THE ROMANS CAME FROM INDIA.

BLING!

BLING! BLING! A term synonymous with expensive jewelry and its accoutrements that celebrates living the good life. With today's media fixated on the lavish lifestyles of our celebrities, we tend to forget that bling has always existed—from the days of early humankind stringing together some gold nuggets, feathers, and bones to today's diamond-encrusted spinner medallions, rose-gold grills, and ice-covered watches. Bling is a visual declaration of financial and stylistic freedom.

THINK YOU KNOW BLING?

Well, **THINK AGAIN** as we present the many definitions of a word that embodies what luxury and wealth look like. So the next time you are at one of those hipster parties and want to impress folks with how cool you are, drop this knowledge on 'em.

DEFINITIONS OF BLING
ACCORDING TO URBANDICTIONARY.COM

bling **1.** Jamaican slang that has been adopted by some African-American rappers and inserted into popular culture. The term "bling bling" refers to the imaginary "sound" that is produced from light reflected by a diamond. **2.** Synonym for expensive, often flashy jewelry sported mostly by African-American hip-hop artists and middle-class Caucasian adolescents. **v.** To "bling-bling;" the act of sporting jewelry of a highly extravagant, gaudy nature. "Damn Orlo, you sure be bling-blinging it tonight!" **n.** "Man, I gots tha bling-bling, yo." **3.** A term for shiny accessories such as chrome wheels, diamonds, etc. **n.** "You know you be lovin' my bling bling!"

Bling Factoids

As it relates to hip-hop, "bling, bling" was allegedly coined in the late '90s by BG of the Cash Money Millionaires, who said upon seeing the 2000 NBA championship ring for the Los Angeles Lakers, "I saw the word 'bling bling' written in diamonds on it. I just wish that I'd trademarked it."

christmas greetings

BOB MARLEY & THE WAILERS

THE SILVERTONES

AL & THE VIBRATIONS

ALTON ELLIS

JENNIFER LARA

JIMMY TUCKER

J.D. SMOOTHE

HORACE ANDY

TOOTS & THE MAYTALS

ROY RICHARDS

THE CABLES

from studio one
reggae • ska
1 STUDIO

See the Silvertones' reggae tune "Bling Bling Christmas" (mid-1960s) for the earliest known usage of the slang.

< Furthering the influence of bling is Mr. T, who set the tone for hip-hop with his thick "dookie ropes," a conscious expression of his African heritage. Bling has since become synonymous not just with jewelry in hip-hop culture, but with anything that expresses wealth to the highest degree.

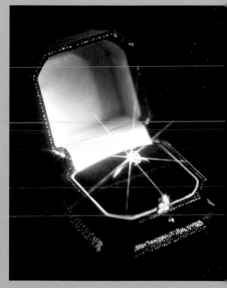

The term "bling bling" refers to the imaginary "sound" that is produced from light reflected by a diamond.

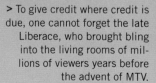 > To give credit where credit is due, one cannot forget the late Liberace, who brought bling into the living rooms of millions of viewers years before the advent of MTV.

Bling Timeline

1970
MANNY'S OF NEW YORK OPENS IN THE DIAMOND DISTRICT, CATERING TO AN EXCLUSIVE CLIENTELE CONSISTING OF MEMBERS OF THE HELLS ANGELS AND HARLEM'S NOTORIOUS DRUG DEALERS SUCH AS LEROY "NICKY" BARNES.

1974
BISHOP DON JUAN FOUNDS THE ANNUAL PLAYER'S BALL IN CHICAGO.

MID TO LATE '70s
THE RISE AND FALL OF HARLEM'S FINEST KINGPIN, LEROY "NICKY" BARNES. HIS TASTE IN EXQUISITE JEWELRY CEMENTS BLING'S PLACE IN THE NEW YORK CITY UNDERGROUND.

1978
TV'S *DALLAS* CELEBRATES THE BLING LIFESTYLE.

LATE '70s
DJ KOOL HERC INTRODUCES HIP-HOP TO THE WORLD. THE B-BOY IS BORN.

1981
DYNASTY COMES ON THE SCENE, FURTHER EXPANDING ON THE BLING LIFESTYLE INTRODUCED BY *DALLAS*.

1983
SCARFACE, THE SEMI-NAL GANGSTER MOVIE THAT INTRODUCED TO HIP-HOP CULTURE THE CONCEPT "GET RICH OR DIE TRYIN'."

1983
LIFESTYLES OF THE RICH AND FAMOUS. ROBIN LEACH IS THE O.G. OF MTV'S *CRIBS*.

1984
MIAMI VICE BRINGS SEX, DRUGS, AND FASHION TO THE MTV GENERATION.

EARLY '90s
DRIVEN BY THE ANTI-APARTHEID MOVEMENT AND A REACTION TO THE EXCESS OF '80S MATERIALISM, CONSCIOUS RAPPERS SPORT LEATHER AFROCENTRIC MEDALLIONS INSTEAD OF GOLD CHAINS AND PENDANTS.

1999
BG OF THE CASH MONEY MILLIONAIRES COINS THE TERM "BLING, BLING" ON THE *CHOPPER CITY IN THE GHETTO* ALBUM. THE TERM BECOMES SYNONYMOUS WITH HIP-HOP JEWELRY.

MID '90s TO PRESENT
BLING IS KING!

the **DAY**

DIAMONDS ARE FORMED UNDER EXTREME HEAT AND PRESSURE DEEP IN THE EARTH'S CRUST
AND COME TO THE SURFACE THROUGH VOLCANIC ERUPTIONS.

BACK IN THE DAYS
WHERE THE
PEOPLE WERE
fresh...

—Kurtis Blow

It's amazing how **"DIPPED"** (i.e., dressed up) one could get with limited dough during the old-school era. Cats came out of the woodwork with their own styles: pinstripe Lee jeans, suede-front shirts, Kangols, British Walkers, Bally shoes, Pumas, Adidas, Cazal eyewear, all adorned with bling of the day, from name-plate belt buckles to silver and gold chains holding up the classic Madonna-with-child medallion piece. It didn't take much to make you official. It wasn't about the size of your rocks, but about how you flipped it. Bling flowed from the attitude, rawness, and creativity bred in the urban streets. As the paid-in-full era rolled through, we started to express the excess from the street economy in the form of truck jewelry, rope "dookie" chains, doorknocker earrings, name rings . . . we did it and we did it BIG! We paused for a minute when Chuck D commanded us to fight the power, got our high-top fades modeled after African kings and queens of centuries past. And let's not forget our leather African medallions, which repped our too black, too strong and "Free South Africa" sentiments. It's time to take a trip down memory lane and look at how we rocked it back then . . .

KURTIS
BLOW

TITO OF
MANNY'S
OF NEW
YORK

TITO THE O.G. ECUADORIAN

ito is the current owner of Manny's of New York, a booth located in New York's famed diamond district. His father, Manny, an established jeweler in Ecuador by the age of 19, immigrated to the States during the 1960s. Upon arriving in New York, he opened a shop on Canal Street in Chinatown. Manny quickly decided he would cater to a specific clientèle, a clientèle who had eccentric tastes with regard to jewelry. In addition, he made it known that he was open to all races, as most of the jewelers in the district at the time did not want to associate with blacks or Latinos. Even though he didn't advertise, business grew exponentially via word of mouth, and Manny landed some loyal customers: primarily members of the Hells Angels and underworld affiliates of famed Harlem drug kingpin Nicky Barnes. Eventually, Manny started attracting his first celebrity clients, professional wrestlers such as Freddie Blassie and Jimmy "Superfly" Snuka. According to Tito, "The wrestlers favored pinkie rings."

Fascinated with jewelry for as long as he could remember, Tito started working with his father in late 1970s. Manny and Tito proved to be a successful team, drawing attention from some of the biggest rap stars in the early days of hip-

TITO WITH BIGGIE

TITO WITH JAY-Z

TITO WITH LL COOL J

hop, such as Kid 'N Play, Eric B. & Rakim, Biz Markie, and LL Cool J, who sported some of Tito's original work during his "Momma Said Knock You Out" era. The large four-finger ring spelling out his name is Tito's design. Tito also serviced Jay-Z (before he had a major record deal), the Notorious B.I.G., Tupac, Heavy D, P. Diddy, Foxy Brown, Cam'ron, Nas, Aaliyah, Noreaga, and Dame Dash. In 1984, Manny moved to a location in Harlem and Tito took over the original Manny's, where he has been ever since. In summing up the high points of a career spanning over thirty years, Tito states, "Whenever an artist or potential client walks into my shop humming or singing my name from a line written by Biggie, Jay-Z, or Noreaga, that's priceless."

One of the many trends Manny's set in motion during the 1970s is the dog tag. Today, major designers like Cartier and Tiffany are finally jumping on the bandwagon and have created their own dog tag lines. Another of Tito's original designs

TITO WITH TUPAC

TITO WITH P DIDDY

TITO WITH LIL' KIM

is the "bone line," worn by Shyne on his most recent album cover. He was also one of the first to dress up watches and create all-diamond bezel-like settings for necklaces. When asked whom he would like to work with in the future, Tito states, "Jay-Z, especially since he was one of the first (if not the first) to mention me in a song ("Politics As Usual," from *Reasonable Doubt*, 1996). Jennifer Lopez, since she's representing the Hispanic community. I'd also like to make something for 50 Cent. His jewelry, especially his spinner medallion, carries the spirit envisioned by my dad when he established this business. Hip-hop was created by the streets for the streets, and now that it is being heard worldwide, rappers are able to afford some fine jewelry. I love it when I'm able to assist a successful artist in expressing and celebrating their success. I enjoy creating original pieces." When asked what bling means to him, Tito says, "Bling is a form of self-expression, regardless of whether one is wearing jewelry or not."

TITO CLASSICS

MTV ONLINE GETS
ITS BLING ON.

A TRULY REMARKABLE PIECE MADE FOR A 1980s BIG WILLIE.

UNTIL THE EIGHTEENTH CENTURY, INDIA WAS THE ONLY KNOWN SOURCE OF DIAMONDS, AND THEY
WERE BELIEVED TO BE ONLY IN THE FABLED MINES OF GOLCONDA.

CLASSIC
PIECES
FROM THE
'80s.

A TRADEMARKED
PIECE DESIGNED
BY TITO'S FATHER,
MANNY.

.45 CALIBER
PISTOL
HANDLES
W/DIAMOND
INLAYS
CUSTOM-MADE
FOR A
WEALTHY
ENTREPRENEUR
FROM
COLOMBIA.

TRUCK JEWELRY

It was the 1980s and it was time to live large and in charge. *New Jack City* was in full effect not only in NYC but in every city across the fifty states. Suzuki Samurais, Jeeps, and VW Jettas tore shit up in the streets. Eric B. & Rakim had soul, Boogie Down Productions beefed with the Juice Crew, and Kane got raw. Girlies rocked biker shorts, and the bling of the day was fat gold chains, aka dookie ropes or cables: Truck jewelry! Everything was big. Super DJ (and producer) Clark Kent (who knows everything you ever need to know about music) explained why they called it *truck*.

"MAN, IT'S CAUSE THAT SHIT WAS SO BIG, LIKE A TRUCK!!!"

Got it, Clark.

BIG
DADDY
KANE
KING ASIATIC
REIGNS SUPREME.
'NUFF SAID.

GHOSTFACE
SLICK RICK'S HEIR APPARENT TO THE KING OF BLING CROWN. HIS BLING IS FLY LIKE AN EAGLE. PEEP THE FRITOS.

SLICK RICK
THE RULER IS
DEFENDING HIS CROWN
BY ANY MEANS NECESSARY.
DON'T TEST HIM!

EPMD
BLING BUSINESS AS
USUAL. PARRISH SMITH
& ERICK SERMON.
ANOTHER B-BOY CLASSIC.

ERIC B
& RAKIM
PAID IN FULL—
REPRESENTING
TRUCK!!!
DON'T SWEAT THEIR
TECHNIQUE.

BIZ MARKIE

RUN-DMC

THE KINGS OF ROCK. THERE ARE
NONE HIGHER. IT ALL STARTED
HERE. PEACE TO JAM MASTER JAY.

MANY OF THE WORLD'S DIAMONDS COME FROM AFRICA, WHERE REBEL GROUPS HAVE USED
THEM TO FUND THEIR CIVIL WARS IN ANGOLA, SIERRA LEONE, LIBERIA, AND THE DEMOCRATIC
REPUBLIC OF CONGO. THESE ARE KNOWN AS "CONFLICT" OR "BLOOD" DIAMONDS.

AFRIKA
BAMBAATAA
ZUUULUUU! THE
FOUNDATION OF HIP-HOP.

FIGHT THE POWER

The late 1980s and early 1990s got real serious. Crack cocaine had devastated 'hoods across the country, apartheid was holding South Africa firmly in its grasp, and Rodney King blessed us by getting that ass beat royally on video. Public Enemy instructed us to "Fight the Power," and X-Clan pointed "To the East Backwards." The hip-hop nation was fed up with all that nonsense and decided to get conscious, and it showed in our jewelry. Black medallions, no gold, yo!

MELLE MEL
TAKES IT BACK OR
"BAT" TO AFRICA.

KRS-ONE

DON'T KNOW WHO THESE DUDES ARE, BUT THEY ARE DEFINITELY KEEPING IT BLACK.

DE LA SOUL
NATIVE TONGUES WITH
B.U.D.D.Y. ON THEIR MIND.

GOLD

Pure gold is twenty-four karat, or 99.999 percent pure. One hundred percent pure gold is nearly impossible to refine.

Gold is a yellow metal. Its chemical symbol is Au, from Aurora, or dawn. The weight of gold or gold articles is usually expressed in troy ounces. (one troy ounce = 1.097 ordinary ounces.) The purity of gold articles is generally described in one of three ways: percent (parts of gold per hundred), fineness (parts of gold per thousand), or karats (parts of gold per twenty-four).

ADDING ALLOYS SUCH AS NICKEL OR PALLADIUM CREATES WHITE GOLD.

Gold is a very dense metal. Its density of 19.32 g/cm3 gives it a very heavy atomic weight, 196.9665, which is why solid gold jewelry is so heavy.

ROSE AND PINK GOLD ARE MADE BY ADDING VARIOUS AMOUNTS OF COPPER—THE MORE COPPER, THE DEEPER THE EFFECT.

ADDING SILVER TO GOLD MAKES GREEN GOLD.

THE WORLD'S DENTISTS USE OVER SIXTY TONS OF GOLD EVERY YEAR.

Gold is marked 24k, 22k, 18k, 14k, or 10k, with the k standing for karat, the system used to describe the proportion of pure gold an item contains.

The oldest gold jewelry ever was crafted in Africa (3,200 B.C.).

AFRICA'S GOLD DEPOSITS WERE FORMED SOME 3.4 BILLION YEARS AGO.

An estimated ten billion tons of gold is suspended in the seas of the world.

Gold has been used as currency for over 5,000 years.

All the gold ever mined in the world would fit into a storeroom measuring seventeen meters long, seventeen meters high, and seventeen meters wide (about 5,000 cubic meters). More steel is poured in an hour than gold has been poured since the beginning of time.

THE LARGEST GOLD NUGGET EVER DISCOVERED WEIGHED 70.92 KILOGRAMS (APPROXIMATELY 160 POUNDS) AND WAS FOUND IN VICTORIA, AUSTRALIA.

The American Federal Reserve on Wall Street, in New York, is the biggest repository of gold in the world; some thirteen thousand tons of gold are kept behind ninety-ton steel doors in vaults blasted out of solid granite.

INDIA HAS BY FAR THE BIGGEST ANNUAL OFFTAKE OF GOLD: 508 TONS IN 1996, ENOUGH TO MAKE ABOUT 175 MILLION PLAIN, 18 CARAT WEDDING RINGS.

A three-inch cube of gold can be hammered so thin that it will cover an acre of ground.

One ounce of gold can be drawn into five miles (eight kilometers) of gold wire. Gold is used in the electronics industry to make more than ten billion tiny electrical contacts every year.

GOLD HAS MEDICINAL AND HEALING PROPERTIES: IT RAISES THE BODY'S METABOLISM BY PROMOTING SMOOTH BLOOD CIRCULATION. GOLD ALSO PREVENTS INFLAMMATION; EVEN TODAY IT IS USED TO TREAT RHEUMATOID ARTHRITIS, CHRONIC ULCERS, AND TUBERCULOSIS.

IT TAKES APPROXIMATELY THREE TONS OF MINED ORE TO YIELD ONE OUNCE OF GOLD.

Gold is found in minute proportions in the human body, whether you have eaten it or not.

Gold is virtually indestructible. Only a few chemicals will attack gold, thus a piece will usually last for many centuries. The spacecraft Voyager, launched in 1977 to explore Saturn then travel away into space forever carries a plate engraved with words and pictures describing the planet earth as we know it, in case it was discovered by another civilization on a distant planet. No wonder the plate is gold; NASA wanted to use the most durable metal possible.

Gold can be eaten. Edible gold leaf, known as Kin-no-mai (fluttering of gold), is widely used for food decoration not only in traditional Japanese cuisine but also in Chinese and Western cuisines. In the past, Chinese consumed gold as an elixir of life (antiaging agent), and in Europe, gold was taken as a special cure for spleen infections. At present, the standard method of eating gold is as gold-leaf decorations on food. Gold is available as furikake, which is seasoned sprinkles for rice, and in sheet form, in spray form, and even in the shape of letters.

Shout-outs to: www.jewelry.about.com, www.goldmartinc.com, www.geotemps.com/goldfacts.html, www.indygem.com, http://smt.blogs.com/japanese_food/2004/08/eat_gold_pika_p.html

LL COOL J
HE'S BAAAAD! UNCLE L STRIKES A BATTLE POSE WITH HIS DOUBLE DOOKIE ROPE. A B-BOY CLASSIC.

BEFORE AND AFTER

THE SUPERSTARS WE KNOW AND LOVE WEREN'T ALWAYS SO BLINGED OUT, AND WE'VE GOT THE PHOTOS TO PROVE IT

("I GOT THE PICTURES, I SEEN YA!").

SO WE TAKE A STROLL DOWN MEMORY LANE TO STARE & LOOK AT HOW SOME CONNOISSEURS BACK IN THE DAY AND THAT FOR CERTAIN, PUT IN WORK!!!

FAT JOE

BEFORE
HERE WE HAVE A BABY-FACED
"FLOW JOE" ROCKING AN ILL MADONNA
WITH CHILD THROWBACK PIECE.

AFTER
"JOEY CRACK"—LARGE AND IN CHARGE WITH HIS
SIGNATURE TERROR SQUAD MEDALLION CAUSING
PHOTOGRAPHERS TO "LEAN BACK."

SLICK RICK

BEFORE

ON THE COME UP, MC RICKY D TAKING A PAGE
FROM THE PREPPY HANDBOOK ON HIS WAY TO
RECORD "HEY YOUNG WORLD."

AFTER

SLICK RICK THE RULER! SHOWS WHY
HE IS THE PAST, PRESENT, AND FUTURE
KING OF BLING.

BUSTA RHYMES

BEFORE
THE PAST HAS NO FUTURE.

AFTER
LOOK MA, NO L.O.N.S!

JERMAINE DUPRI

BEFORE
A YOUNG JERMAINE DUPRI WITH HIS BLING
STARTER KIT. HE'S HERE TO MAKE YOU
JUMP! JUMP!

AFTER
MONEY AIN'T A THANG WHEN IT COMES
TO HIS BLING BLING: ROCKING AN
ASSORTMENT OF BEJEWELED PIECES.

thre

The

ON MAY 13, 1888, USING A PEN ENCRUSTED WITH DIAMONDS AND EMERALDS, THE IMPERIAL REGENT
PRINCESS DOÑA ISABEL SIGNED THE DECREE ENDING SLAVERY IN BRAZIL. WITH A SINGLE STROKE, SHE
LIBERATED 1,500,000 MEN, WOMEN, AND CHILDREN, AND BROUGHT FREEDOM TO THE LAST SLAVE-HOLDING
COUNTRY IN THE WESTERN HEMISPHERE.

e

ICE AGE

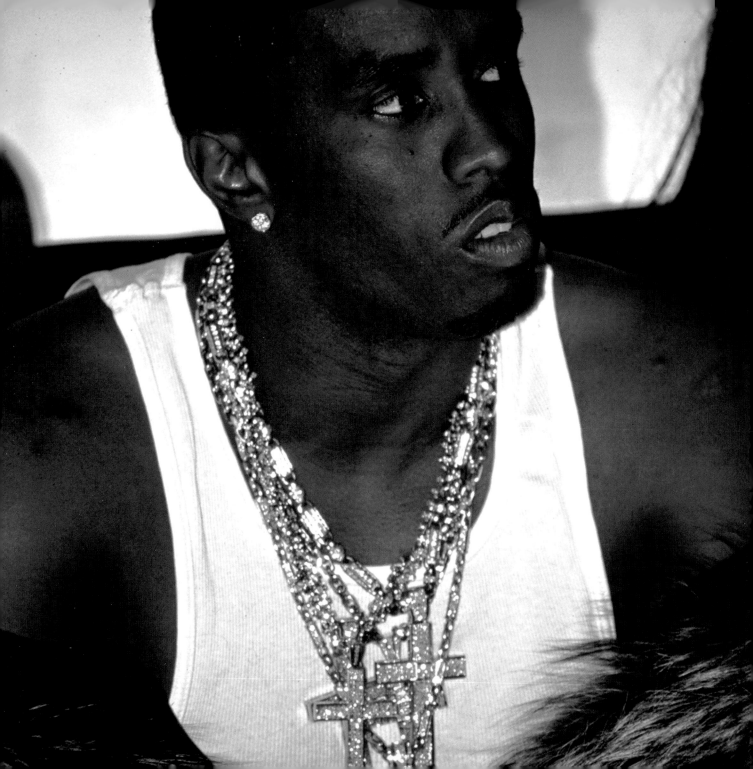

IF TRUCK JEWELRY REPRESENTED HIP-HOP'S GOLDEN AGE DURING THE MID TO LATE 1980s, PLATINUM AND *Diamonds* USHERED IN THE ICE AGE.

If truck jewelry represented hip-hop's golden age—the mid- to late 1980s—platinum and diamonds ushered in the ice age. Never had our culture experienced such affluence—and mainstream acceptance. Gold became passé as artists like Puff Daddy, Jay-Z, Master P, and Cash Money Millionaires began achieving multiplatinum status on a consistent basis. (In the recording industry, a record is deemed "gold" when it sells over five hundred thousand units and "platinum" when it sells over one million.)

In celebration of being admitted into the platinum club, artists made the world take note of their new status with watches, rings, earrings, and chains. As Jigga rapped on "Ride or Die," featured on his most-successful-to-date *Vol. 2 . . . Hard Knock Life* (1998), "Time to separate the platinum from the white gold, right from the door."

LIL' KIM
KIM ROCKS HER "TREASURE" CHEST!

DIAMONDS ARE A GIRL'S BEST FRIEND.

LUDACRIS
LUDA SHOWS OFF HIS SKULL PIECE
MODELED BY ANTON THE MODELER.
GUARANTEED TO WARD OFF
EVIL SPIRITS, WACK RAPPERS, AND
BILL O'REILLY.

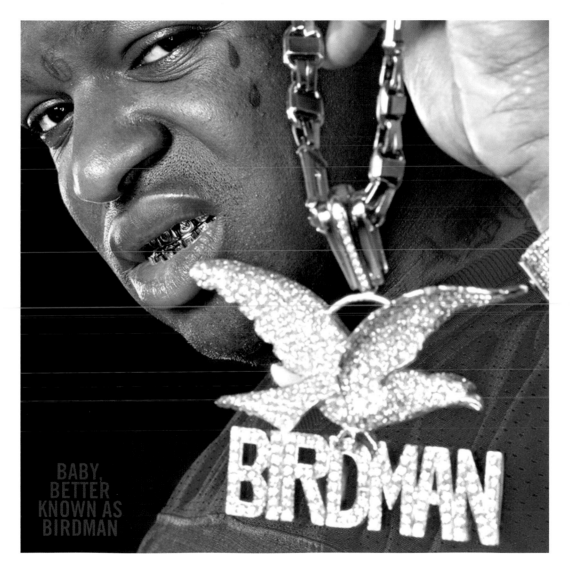

BABY,
BETTER
KNOWN AS
BIRDMAN

THE METRIC CARAT, WHICH EQUALS 0.2 GRAMS, IS THE STANDARD UNIT OF WEIGHT FOR DIAMONDS AND MOST OTHER
GEMS. IF OTHER FACTORS ARE EQUAL, THE MORE A STONE WEIGHS, THE MORE VALUABLE IT WILL BE.

LLIONAIRE   YS CLUB

PHARRELL
DUDE, LIKE, WHERE'S MY
SKATEBOARD. OH YEAH,
ON MY NECK.

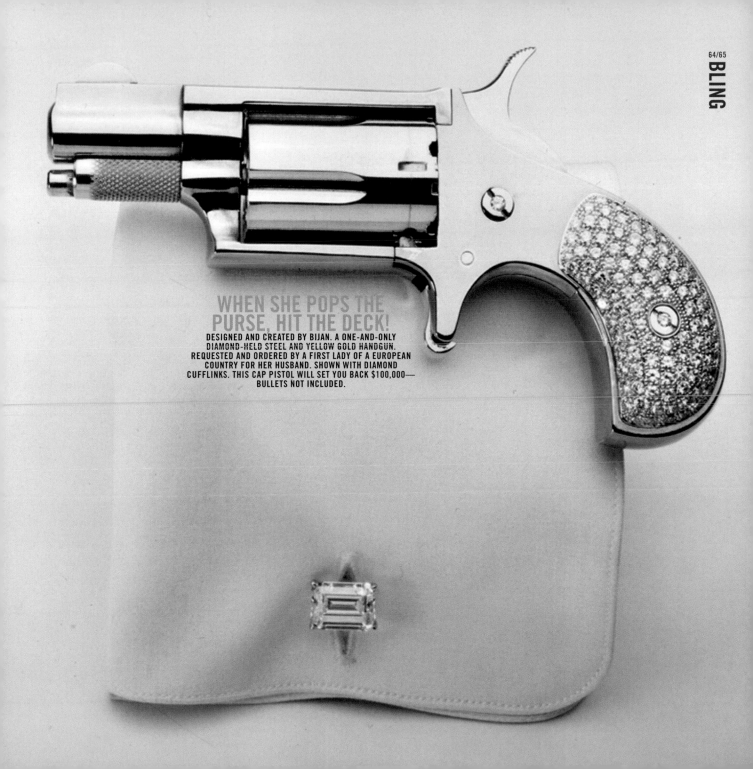

WHEN SHE POPS THE PURSE, HIT THE DECK!
DESIGNED AND CREATED BY BIJAN. A ONE-AND-ONLY DIAMOND-HELD STEEL AND YELLOW GOLD HANDGUN. REQUESTED AND ORDERED BY A FIRST LADY OF A EUROPEAN COUNTRY FOR HER HUSBAND. SHOWN WITH DIAMOND CUFFLINKS. THIS CAP PISTOL WILL SET YOU BACK $100,000— BULLETS NOT INCLUDED.

NELLY
SHOWS US HOW MANY MORE
PIECES OF BLING HE SHOULD
HAVE WORN FOR THE DAY.

Rangs an' Thangs

You know someone has their pimp game straight by the pinkie ring they floss. The right piece will light up a room and draw

all types of attention, from the admirers, the haters, and everyone in between. Here are some rings both past and present

that bear testimony to the importance of being the Lord of the Ring.

GHOSTFACE
GET IT RIGHT: IT'S
G.H.O.S.T.

LL COOL J
LL SHOWCASING CUSTOM-MADE PIECES BY TITO. HE'S BAAAD!

BISHOP DON
"MAGIC" JUAN
BISHOP'S RING GAME IS TIGHT AS EVER BUT
YO, WASSUP WITH THE MANICURE?

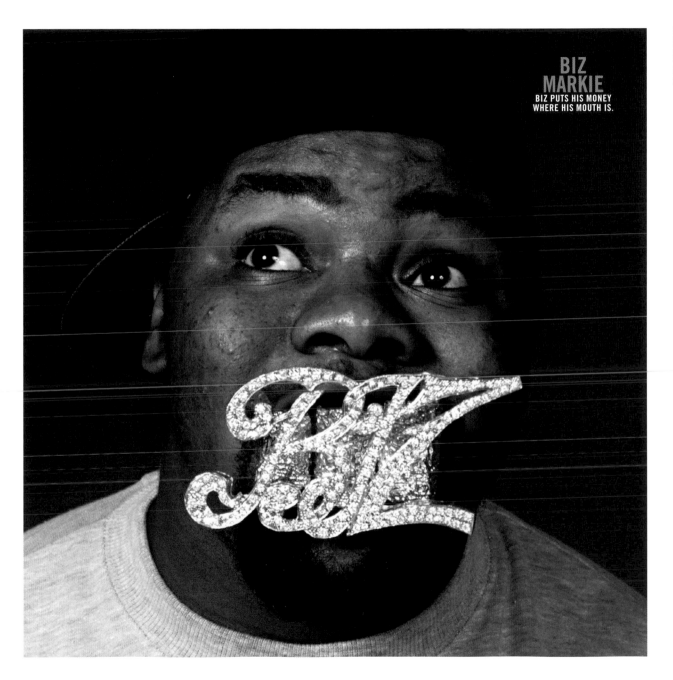

**BIZ
MARKIE**
**BIZ PUTS HIS MONEY
WHERE HIS MOUTH IS.**

GEMSTONES

It has been proven that wealth kept in this form of capital investment can survive inflation better than any other investments.

EMERALDS

Emerald is a valuable gemstone that symbolizes love and success. It is May's birthstone and the anniversary gemstone for the twentieth year of marriage.

The first emerald mines were in Egypt. Mummies were often buried with an emerald on their neck carved with the symbol for foliage, to symbolize eternal youth.

It was recorded that Nero watched his gladiator games through flat emerald crystals.

Pliny, the Roman scholar, was the first to suggest emerald was a family member of beryl. It was not until the early nineteenth century that science proved him right.

THE ROMANS DEDICATED THE EMERALD TO THEIR GODDESS OF LOVE AND BEAUTY, VENUS.

IT IS SAID THAT CLEOPATRA WAS ALWAYS ADORNED IN EMERALDS AND HAD AMASSED AN ASTOUNDING COLLECTION OF THIS GEM, WHICH ADORNED HER MOST TREASURED JEWELRY.

The emerald was known in ancient times not only for its beauty but also for its alleged power of healing diseases, strengthening memory, increasing intelligence, and inspiring eloquence.

Rubies and sapphires are closely related and are formed from the same substance, corundum.

Most rubies are mined in Southeast Asia, in Myanmar (formerly known as Burma), Thailand, and Vietnam, and in Madagascar. More than 90 percent of the world's rubies come from Myanmar. In 2003 the U.S. banned imports from Myanmar to protest the government's human rights violations.

RUBIES

Star rubies (like star sapphires) are cabochon cut and show a six-legged star in the dome. The star should stand out clearly, and each leg should be equally prominent.

RUBIES ARE THE BIRTHSTONE FOR JULY.

EXTREMELY RARE AND EXPENSIVE, RUBIES RANGE IN COLOR FROM PINKISH TO BLOOD RED.

SAPPHIRES

Sapphire, September's birthstone, has been the preeminent blue gemstone for centuries. Ancient Persian rulers believed its reflection painted the heavens blue. Indeed, its very name in Latin, sapphirus, means blue.

While sapphire has become the ultimate blue stone, it actually comes in almost every color except red (red sapphires are rubies), including colorless and white, and such fancy colors as yellow, peach, orange, cognac, pink, violet, purple, and green, and all their many shades.

SAPPHIRE IS KNOWN AS THE STONE OF PROSPERITY.

According to one version of the book of Exodus, Yahweh gave Moses the Ten Commandments on tablets of sapphire. Sapphire has historically been associated with the sacred and divine, a guardian of innocence and bestower of truth. This gem was believed to attract divine favor to its owner.

Sapphires were used as talismans to protect travelers, ward off illness, and bring peace, joy, and wisdom.

WHITE SAPPHIRE HAS BECOME A POPULAR DIAMOND SUBSTITUTE. IT'S A GREAT CHOICE FOR AN ENGAGEMENT RING. IN FACT, THE RING PRINCE CHARLES GAVE TO LADY DIANA WAS A SAPPHIRE, NOT A DIAMOND.

Among the most famous sapphires are two of the world's largest. The Smithsonian Institute in Washington, D.C., houses the Logan sapphire, a 423-carat cushion-cut stone from Sri Lanka that is set in a brooch surrounded by diamonds. The second is the 258-carat bright blue sapphire from the Russian crown, kept in the Diamond Fund in Moscow.

AVIANNE & CO.
The Youngest Ones In Charge!

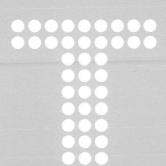

here's been a lot of talk about these new guys: Avi, Joey, Izzy, Arsen, and Gabriel of Avianne & Co. Besides the fact that their jewelry is hot, the word is that these guys are the young guns of NYC's diamond district (the oldest one is 27), conquering 47th Street. Brothers Avi and Joey grew up with their sights on something far from jewelry: they were training to be on the United States Olympic judo team. As the Olympics came and went, the brothers, along with their cousins, decided it was time they became involved in the family business, jewelry. Avianne & Co. opened shop in early 2000 and was almost automatically accepted by a vast clientèle of celebrity blingsters. As Avi puts it, "Before I opened shop, I was very good friends with the late, great Jam Master Jay. He always told me that if I ever needed him, he was a phone call away. The minute I went into business, I called Jay, and he came through like he said he would." Since then, Avianne & Co. has handled a lot of hip-hop clientele: Just Blaze, 50 Cent and the entire G-Unit clique, the Game, Cam'ron, the Diplomats, State Property, Jamie Foxx, Ronald Isley, and B2K, to name a few. Their first custom piece was made for Jagged Edge: the definitive Jagged Edge logo for their chests. It was typical of Avianne's work: a lot of preparation and client consultation. "We sit with the client and start with an idea, then we produce a

drawing, then we use the drawing against wax to model our work, then we go to production in metal, so designing jewelry is truly a step-by-step process . . . We don't just do pieces, we create. There's a lot of love that goes into our pieces. It's like raising a baby, and we raise our child like there's no tomorrow." It's a process that leads to friendships with clients and, not surprisingly, some envy among other jewelers. "I stopped putting my merchandise in the window since the other cats will copy your shit immediately," Avi says. "I understand the frustration that some of the other jewelers may feel. Man, there's fifteen thousand jewelers on this block, on this one block." Some of Avianne & Co.'s more memorable pieces were an exact replica of Black Rob's face, Cam'ron's golf ball earrings for the "Oh Boy" video, and the signature State Property piece for Beanie Sigel and the rest of the State Property crew. As for the most challenging piece, Avi once designed a miniature Rubik's Cube with different-color stones that actually turns like a real Rubik's Cube. "A lot of time, design, and mathematics went into that." When asked why hip-hop has such a strong love affair with bling, Avi says, "Hip-hop is a competitive sport, so it's about who has the biggest, baddest, dopest rhymes. Naturally it extends to who has the biggest, baddest, dopest piece of bling."

IT IS BELIEVED THAT A DIAMOND ENDOWS THE WEARER WITH COURAGE AND FORTITUDE, BRINGS VICTORY AND GOOD
FORTUNE, WARDS OFF EVIL, PROTECTS AGAINST THE PLAGUE, PROMOTES CONSTANCY IN A MARRIAGE.

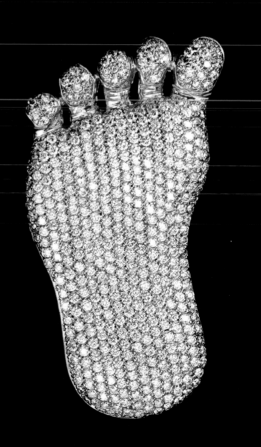

SOUL SISTERS
KNOCK KNOCK! WHO'S THERE?
SOUL SISTERS FINESSE & SYNQUIS
FROM BACK IN THE DAY.

Earrings

Door knockers and dolphin earrings are coming back, not only on our shorties in the hood but all over the place in fashion. It's a reminder of when our hip-hop queens rocked heavy weight on their lobes with pride and dignity. Earrings have played a major role with our blingsters and their bling game. Remember when dudes wouldn't get caught dead with both lobes pierced? Times have changed . . . but our love for the earpieces remains strong.

WHEN JESUS WALKS

One thing about our blingsters—they definitely love Jesus. It's good to see that no matter how hot our stars get, they pay respect. Check out how some of our stars walk with Christ.

JA RULE
CONTEMPLATING HIS
COMEBACK WITH BOTH
COGNAC AND CHRIST IN MIND.

KANYE WEST
MR. "JESUS WALKS" HIMSELF. WITH—
WHAT ELSE?—A JESUS PIECE!

MA$E
JESUS LOVES ME.

four
GRILLS *and*

GOBLETS

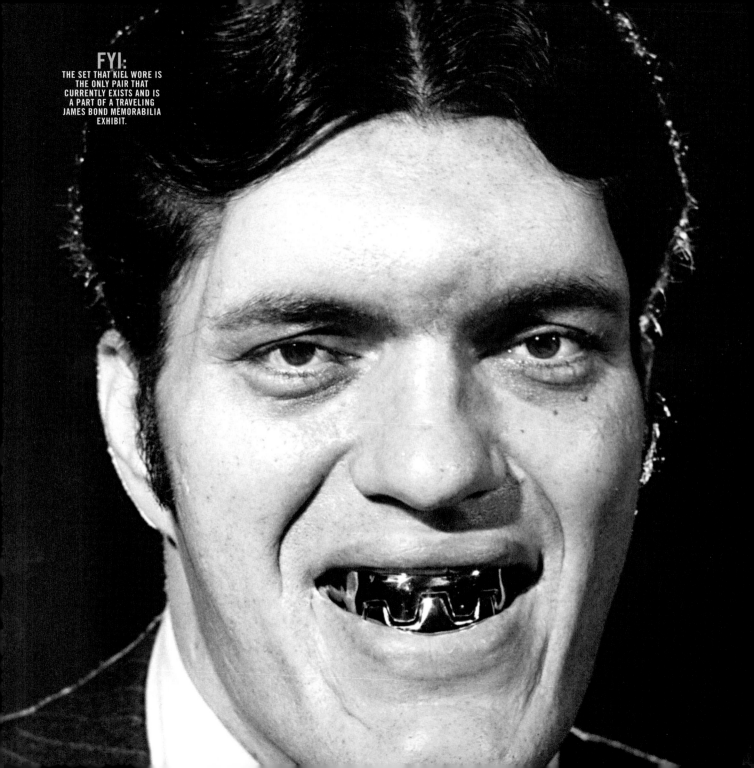

WHO COULD FORGET RICHARD KIEL AS JAWS IN THOSE JAMES BOND FLICKS SPORTING THE CHROMIUM GRILL READY TO CHOMP ON THAT ASS? EVEN 007 HAD TO BACK UP AND RECOGNIZE.

Yo Son,

RESPECT THE GRILL!

AKA GRILLS, FRONTS, AND SLUGS (single teeth)

GOLD TEETH

have always been a status symbol. It was Arculanus (Giovanni d'Arcoli) who, in 1848, first had the idea of using gold for dental fillings. Having gold fillings was a sign of wealth; travelers in a tight spot could even use them as a form of currency. God forbid you were buried with your gold teeth: more than likely a grave robber would relieve you of your fronts, if your undertaker hadn't done so already. Nowadays in hip-hop parlance, "the grill" is slang for a person's mouth or face; the term has been attributed to the elaborate, ornate grills of luxury automobiles. A "grill" involves the bonding of teeth; the first was sighted on the streets of downtown Brooklyn during the toddler years of hip-hop. Just-Ice, Kool G Rap, and Flavor Flav were some of hip-hop's first wearers of the gold fronts. The Dirty South carries on the rich tradition of the grill as seen on Big Gip of Goodie Mob—the first to rock the platinum grills, followed by Baby of the Cash Money Millionaires.

Permanent or removable? A slug of just tops or bottoms? Yellow gold, red gold, or platinum? Iced? Carved designs? Opened? Do you spell "Nasty Nega," like Nas rocks across his teeth in the "Thief's Theme" video, or do you rock some smoothed-out plates, like Master P? The process of selecting the perfect mouthpiece can be as complicated as getting a tattoo. Madonna even rocked a slug in her "Music" video that featured pseudo B-Boy Ali G. And who can forget Brigitte Nielsen passionately locking grills with Flavor Flav on the VH1 reality show *Strange Love*?

Taking off in Queens, Miami, Atlanta, Tennessee, Mississippi, and all the way to Japan, grills are the purchase of choice when it comes to showing off that blinged-out 28k smile and have become a mainstay accessory in the world of bling!

THE RZA

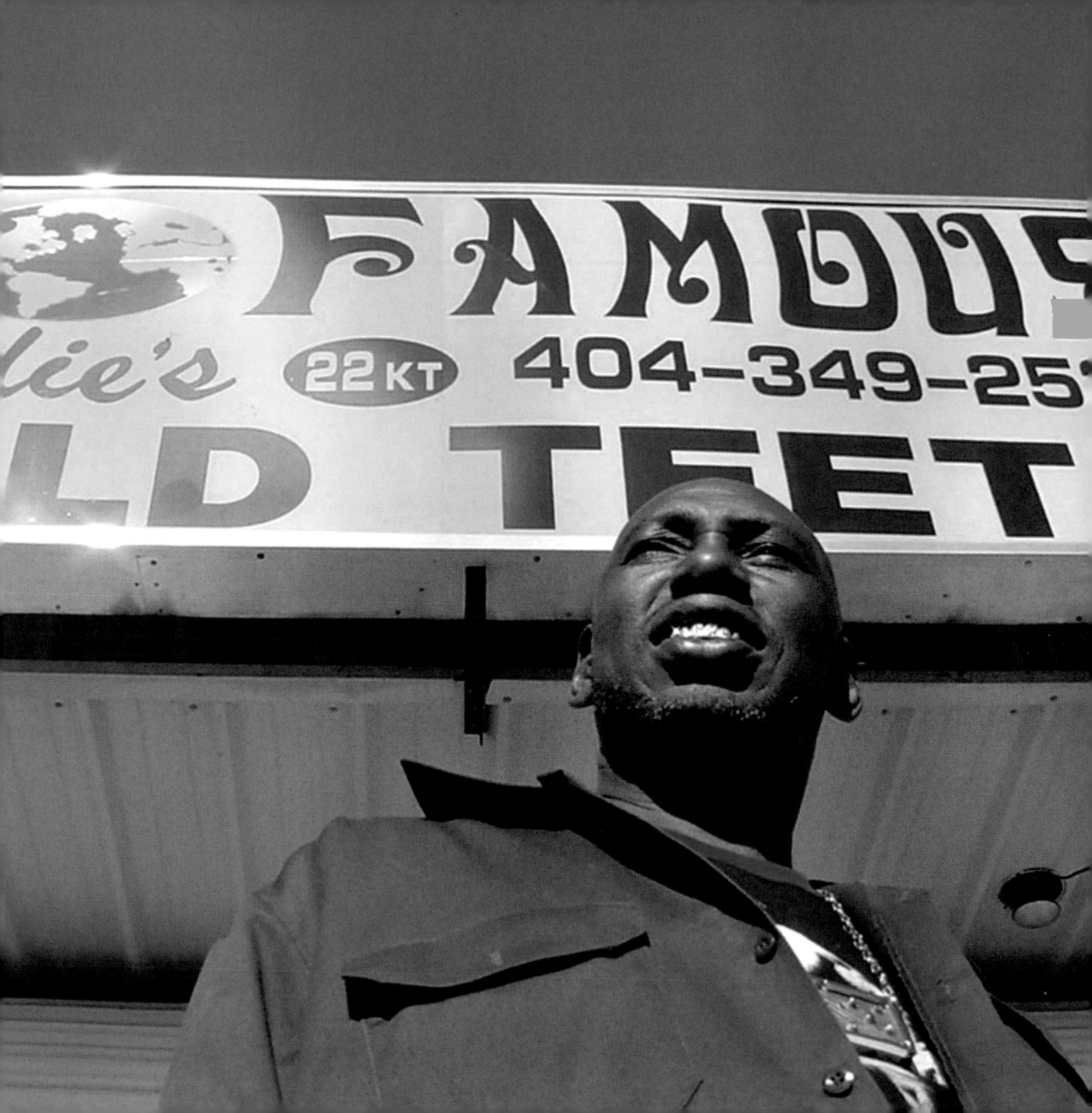
FAMOU
lie's
22KT
404-349-25
LD TEET

EDDIE'S FAMOUS GOLD TEETH
Eddie Plein, the Originator of the Grill

Eddie Plein is known in many circles as the originator of the grill. Born in Suriname, South America, his parents immigrated to Brooklyn in 1971, when he was about 13 years old. Eddie was very familiar with gold teeth as they had been popular in Suriname and other areas of South America, the West Indies, and the southern U.S. for years. Even his mother sported a gold tooth. Eddie enrolled as a student at Queensborough Community College. An avid soccer player, he thought he was destined to become a pro. But during a trip to Suriname in 1981, his first time home in a decade, things changed dramatically. One day, while dining at a restaurant there, he broke his back tooth. The next day, at the dentist, the idea to make gold fronts hit him like a lightening bolt. When he got up from the patient's chair and left the office, he knew that back in the U.S., he would get a dental degree and become a gold-tooth specialist. Immediately after Eddie returned to New York, he left college and enrolled at the Magna Dental Institute and worked in dental labs after school to gain more training and experience. Eddie started experimenting with putting gold teeth together. Gold teeth were already out, but two, three, or four gold teeth bound together was unheard of. Eddie kept mixing and remixing styles until he invented

RECOGNIZE THE REAL...

the removable grill. His "laboratory" was the kitchen of his mother's house. Seeing how skillful he had become, she allowed him to replace her original gold tooth from Suriname, becoming his first client.

Eventually, armed with skill, confidence and a vision of the grill and its potential impact on the landscape of hip-hop, Eddie decided it was time for him to open his first shop. He found a spot at 169th Street and Hillside Avenue in Jamaica, Queens, at a place called Angelica Jewelry, a pawnshop type of operation run by Russians buying and selling gold. During the early 1980s, dentists were the only people doing gold dental work, but the owners let Eddie experiment with a storefront dealing exclusively in gold teeth. He instantly attracted street hustlers like Prince, the 168th and Jamaica Avenue crew, Black Jus, Shaboo, and Tommy Mickens, a.k.a Tommy Montana, all well respected and "made" dudes in the neighborhood. Business instantly took off. Eddie became known not only for his grills but for the personalized designs he would hand cut into his product: stars, hearts, aces, Playboy bunnies. By the mid 1980s Eddie needed a bigger storefront and decided it was time to move.

Eddie found his next storefront at what would soon become a commercial center for hip-hop gear. The Coliseum, a few blocks from Angelica, at Jamaica Avenue and 165th Street, housed three legendary hip-hop shops: Mitch's, a sneaker shop where one could find all of the hottest, most recent flavors in footwear; the legendary Shirt Kings, who

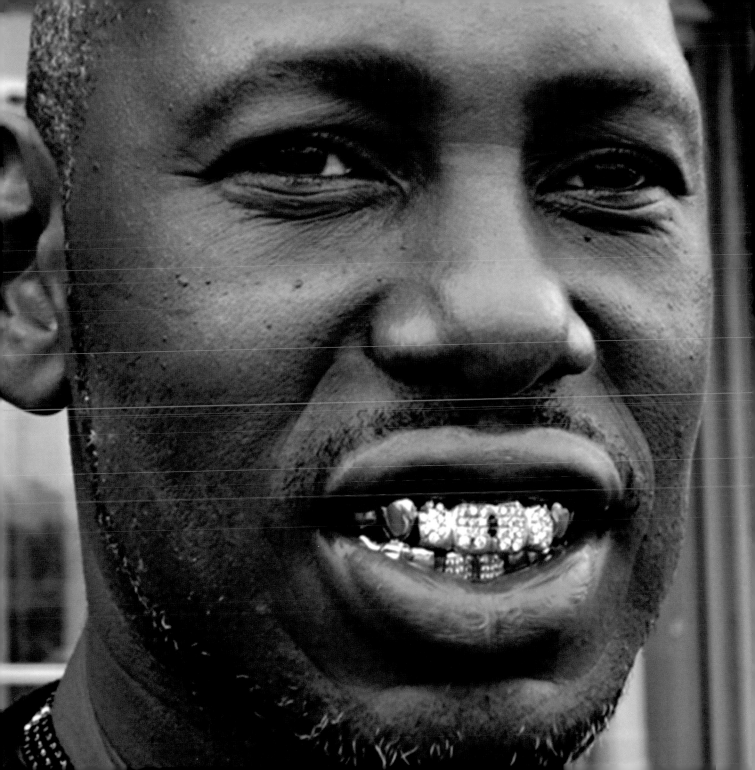

EDDIE AT WORK ON SHANE'S GRILL (BACKGROUND).

EDDIE AT WORK CARVING HIS FAMOUS DESIGNS.

EDDIE AND THE "CLEANERS" FARRELL (LEFT) AND DEZO (RIGHT). A "CLEANER" IS A FINISHER WHO BASICALLY TAKES THE MODELED TEETH AND REMOVES ALL EXCESS EMBELLISHMENT ON THE DESIGN AND THEN DELIVERS A FINISHED PRODUCT.

EDDIE AND LOYAL CUSTOMERS (L-R); FORREST, BT, AND SHANE. EVEN WHITE BOYS GET CRUNK'D IN THE DIRTY DIRTY.

ADVERTISEMENT FOR EDDIE'S GOLD TEETH IN DOWNTOWN ATLANTA @ THE UNDERGROUND.

made and sold custom T-shirts and sweat shirts; and finally, Eddie's Gold Teeth. "We blew the Coliseum up," recalls Eddie. "It was a phenomenon. Everyone followed me from Angelica to the Coliseum. LL Cool J came through, the God Rakim came through. I did Big Daddy Kane's teeth, I did Heavy D's teeth, I did Salt & Pepa's teeth, I did Kool G Rap's teeth right after he recorded 'It's a Demo.'" The first rapper ever to wear Eddie's work was Just-Ice, who ordered two teeth with the initials JS inscribed on them. He wanted them in a hurry: He was performing that night. After Eddie delivered satisfactorily, Just-Ice became a regular. Eddie's work was featured on the cover of every album that Just-Ice recorded. "I started with only two, but eventually I did all thirty-two of Just-Ice's teeth," he says. Another famous client was Flavor Flav. "Flav represented my teeth worldwide."

Toward the end of the 1980s, the "New Jack" era began to fade as Mayor Rudy Giuliani and Governor George Pataki put a choke hold on the drug trade. New York City became a place known less for its high rollers and players and more for its underground grassroots backpackers and daisy-agers, a movement set in motion by groups such as De La Soul, A Tribe Called Quest, Jungle Brothers, Poor Righteous Teachers, and Brooklyn's very own Boot Camp Clik. Business dried up for Eddie as everybody jumped on the bandwagon. "The Chinese started opening up shops and undercut our work by charging dudes sixty dollars for gold teeth," Eddie recalls. "The high rollers and rappers were feeling fucked up since the young boys started sporting cheap-ass gold teeth." Business got so bad that Eddie started moving around,

from New York to Hampton, Virginia, to Baltimore to Miami, where, with his brother, he opened a store. It was in Miami that he and his brother did grills for such stars as Goldie (UK Hip-Hop, INCredible Sound of Drum 'n' Bass DJ and producer), Luther "Luke" Campbell and members of the infamous 2 Live Crew. Sometime after 1992, Eddie relocated to Atlanta, Georgia, setting up his own shop in the famous underground mall known as "The Underground" (a hotbed for urban shoppers looking to get fresh for the weekend). Clientèle poured in from all over—Alabama, Tennessee, Cincinnati, Kentucky, Detroit. Eddie's first clients from the South were Cee-lo, who then introduced him to the Goodie Mob, Outkast, Lil Jon, Ying Yang Twins, Lloyd, and Ludacris.

PRICE INFO FOR EDDIE'S GOLD TEETH
Man on the Street price: $120.00 and up depending upon specification.
Big Balla prices: $12,000–14,000 (which may include princess-cut diamonds, bezels, and either gold or platinum).

JAHVANNIE, ONE OF EDDIE'S CRAFTSMEN, SHOWING HIS SHINY FRONTS. JAWS DOESN'T HAVE ANY- THING ON HIM!

94/95 BLING

Eddie currently remains in Atlanta, where he services most of the dirty dirty's reigning crunk kings. His work not only appears in the many Southern rap videos flooding MTV and BET, but he continues to service many personalities from New York, including Allen Iverson, Kelis, and Nas (check out his video for "Thief's Theme"). "I'm a lucky guy," reflects Eddie. "I made history in New York, a movement, and I made history, created a movement, in the South. I invented something that had never existed before, the world's first removable grill. The removable grill is my baby that I brought into the world and that will go in all of the social studies and history books." One of Eddie's other legacies is that his work once saved a client's life. "I had this dude from South Carolina back in 1999—dude got shot in his mouth, all his gold teeth were cemented in, the bullet went in his mouth and ricocheted all around, knocked all the gold teeth out, and bounced out through a cheek. The doctors in the emergency room told him if he didn't have gold teeth, he would certainly be dead. Eddie's gold teeth done saved niggas' lives."

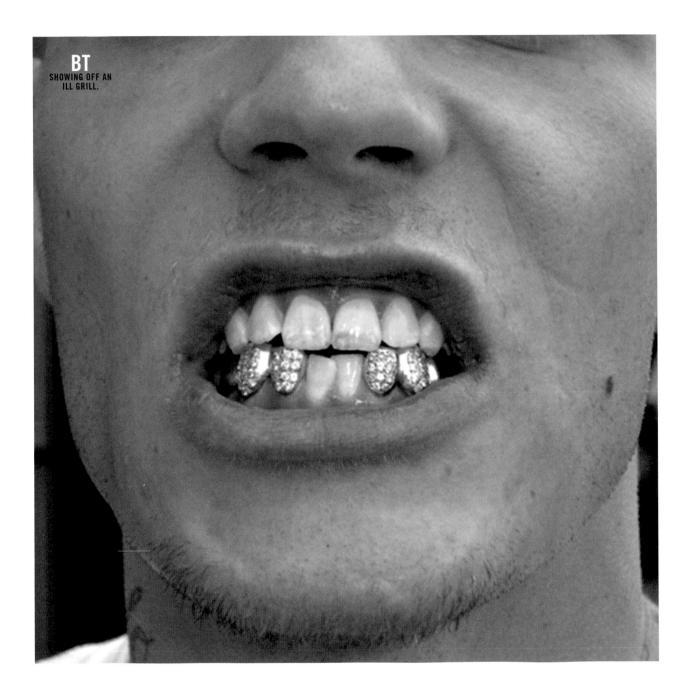

BT
SHOWING OFF AN
ILL GRILL.

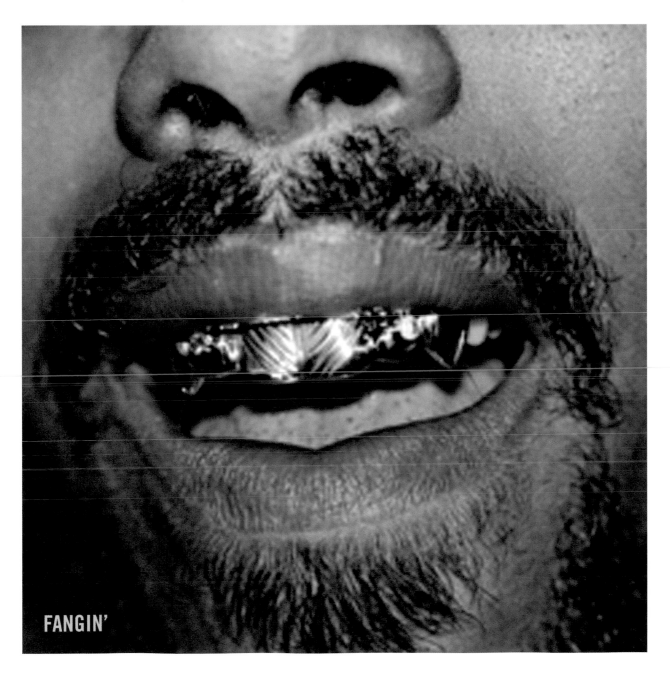

FANGIN'

AHHH...
PLATINUM.

NOT YOUR
GRANDMOTHER'S
TEETH...

ALTHOUGH DIAMONDS ARE PERCEIVED AS A WHITE—ACTUALLY, COLORLESS—GEM, THEY COME IN A SPECTRUM OF COLORS; COLORED DIAMONDS ARE CALLED "FANCIES."

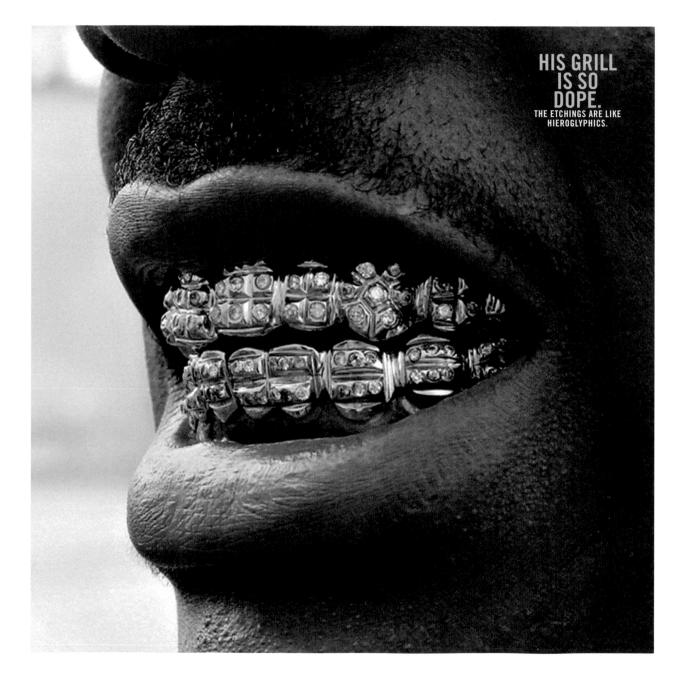

HIS GRILL
IS SO
DOPE.
THE ETCHINGS ARE LIKE
HIEROGLYPHICS.

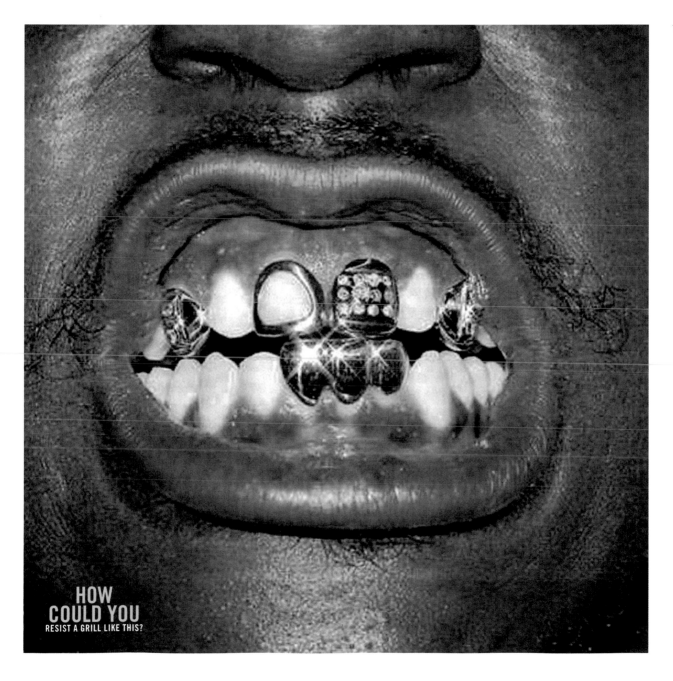

HOW
COULD YOU
RESIST A GRILL LIKE THIS?

TEST YOUR HIP-HOP GRILL SKILLS AND IDENTIFY THE FOLLOWING GRILLS.

IN MEMORIAM

ASON
AKA OLD DIRTY BASTARD
AKA DIRT MCGIRT
AKA BIG BABY JESUS
AKA RUSSELL JONES
AKA ODB
RETURNED TO THE 36 CHAMBERS.
NOV. 15, 1968–NOV. 13, 2004

MUCH LOVE. R.I.P.

PLATINUM

The story of platinum is much longer than most people realize. Some meteorites contain platinum, and the earliest known meteorite impact on Earth happened two billion years ago. The ancient Egyptians, pre-Incan civilizations, and the Spanish conquistadors all encountered platinum. It reemerged in the 1700s to fascinate kings and alchemists alike.

All the platinum ever mined would fit in the average-size living room!

AS IS TRUE OF ALL PRECIOUS METALS, PLATINUM CAN BE SCRATCHED. WITH PLATINUM, HOWEVER, THERE IS NO MATERIAL LOST FROM THE SCRATCH, AS THERE IS WITH GOLD. IF YOUR PLATINUM JEWELRY BECOMES SCRATCHED, SIMPLY TAKE IT TO YOUR JEWELER FOR A QUICK POLISH.

Platinum is the heaviest of the precious metals, weighing almost twice as much as gold. Its strength ideally secures diamonds and other precious gems. The world's famous diamonds, including the Hope, Jonker, and Koh-I-Noor, are secured by the permanence of platinum.

Ten tons of ore must be mined to produce a single ounce of platinum. It takes five months to process platinum ore into pure platinum. Only after that can skilled hands work their craftsmanship, transforming platinum into pieces of wearable art.

Platiunum is used for coating missile nose cones, jet engines, fuel nozzles, etc., which must perform reliably at high temperatures for long periods of time.

PLATINUM WILL NOT WEAR AWAY OR WEAR DOWN. FOR EXAMPLE, AFTER MANY YEARS OF WEAR, A GOLD WEDDING BAND'S SHANK WILL WEAR DOWN AND BECOME THINNER. THIS IS NOT THE CASE WITH A PLATINUM RING.

Platinum reached its peak of popularity in the early 1900's, when it was the preferred metal for all fine jewelry in the U.S. When World War II began, the government declared platinum a strategic metal, and its use in nonmilitary applications, including jewelry, was disallowed. To appease consumers who preferred platinum's white luster, white gold was substituted.

In America, platinum jewelry contains either 90 or 95 percent pure platinum. By comparison, eighteen karat gold is 75 percent pure and fourteen karat is 58 percent pure gold. Platinum will never tarnish or lose its luster.

SILVER

Man learned to separate silver from lead as early as 3,000 BC. Silver has been mined and prized for its beauty and durability for at least six thousand years.

Silver is the best conductor of electricity of all the elements. In fact, silver defines conductivity: All other metals are compared against it. On a scale of zero to one hundred, silver ranks one hundred, with copper at ninety-seven and gold at seventy-six.

Silver has superior bactericidal qualities. Small concentrations of silver or silver salts kill bacteria by chemically affecting the cell membranes, causing them to break down. Bacteria do not develop resistance to silver, as they do to many antibiotics.

SILVER IS THE BEST CONDUCTOR OF HEAT OF ALL THE ELEMENTS. ITS USE IN SOLAR PANELS AND AUTOMOBILE REAR-WINDOW DEFOGGERS TAKES ADVANTAGE OF THIS QUALITY.

About one third of the silver produced worldwide is used in photography.

Silver has the highest degree of optical reflectivity of all the elements. A silver mirror can reflect about 95 percent of the visible-light spectrum (most mirrors are silver). Besides their aid to our vanity, mirrors are important components in telescopes, microscopes, and solar panels.

SILVER IODIDE IS OFTEN USED IN CLOUD SEEDING. A POUND OF SILVER IODIDE IS ENOUGH TO SEED MANY CUBIC MILES OF CLOUDS.

Sterling silver, the best-known alloy of silver, is 92.5 percent fine silver and 7.5 percent copper, by definition.

Shout-out to www.silverusersassociation.org.

Sterling silver will slowly tarnish when exposed to air and moisture. The small amount of copper in the sterling silver alloy is principally responsible for the tarnish. Pure silver tarnishes very little, but it is too soft for jewelry.

DR. MARK JACKSON & DR. RONALD CUNNING aka The Hip-Hop Dentists Precision Ceramics Dental Laboratory

 hile Eddie may be the originator of the gold fronts, there are many others who have staked a claim to this hip-hop fashion statement. On the West Coast, in a quiet suburb north of Los Angeles, lies Precision Ceramics Dental Laboratory. Featured on VH1 and with Master P on *MTV Cribs*, and with Snoop Dogg and his family as regular customers, Precision Ceramics Dental Laboratory has become one of the hottest places to go in the dental industry.

Dr. Mark Jackson recalls how, about six years ago, he and Dr. Roland Cunning got into the business of doing fronts: "Miramax called me up and said, We have this rapper over here with gold teeth, but we have to cover them up and make them look like natural teeth. He asked if we could do something. I said we could give it a try." The next morning, at 6 a.m., Master P rolled into the lab in a bulletproof Chevy Suburban with his entourage. The dentists took impressions of his teeth—permanent gold with diamonds in them—and made theatrical façades of acrylic resin that snapped over them and looked identical to natural teeth. Master P loved them so much that he had another six sets made. (Precision Ceramics keeps a set of Master P's so they can make new ones for him at any time). A couple of days later, Master P's brother C-Murder wanted a removable set made, so he paid a visit to the lab too. But a few months after that, C-Murder came back and complained that the guys were giving him grief, saying his removable pair was "like having a fake tattoo." So he decided he wanted to go for the real thing. Dr. C was hesitant, but Dr. Jackson pulled him aside and said, "Listen, if he was a guy off the street who had crooked or discolored teeth, we would make him some crowns in a second. Where C-Murder comes from, this is cosmetic dentistry. If we don't do it, someone else will—or he'll go back home to Baton Rouge and go to one of those tattoo parlors and get some tin-can crowns, and those aren't healthy. If we do it here, at least we can do it right. And it will last him for the rest of his life. Plus we can always cut them off and put porcelain crowns on and be right back to normal. We'll have his impressions here to know what his teeth looked like before."

Dr. C agreed. The dentists did his six uppers and later his six lower teeth, and had him come back another day to have the rest finished off. It cost $5,000 to $6,000 a tooth for the front teeth with the diamonds in them, and anywhere from $3,000 to $15,000 each for the back teeth. Dr. Jackson says that they do about four sets of teeth a year—and thankfully so.

"When we have celebrities arrive for this kind of work, we have to block off an entrance and close down six operatories and work all night in order to give them their teeth the next day."

One of the strangest requests Precision Ceramics has ever had, Dr. Jackson remembers, was from rapper Slick Rick. He wanted to have his six front teeth encrusted in pavé diamonds like his eye patch so that they would sparkle like a disco ball when he turned his head. The dentists received numerous pictures, sketches, and ideas of what he was looking for. They met with a jeweler to find out how to lay the pavé stones in a hygienic way and also how to be sure the diamonds would be secure in his teeth. Finally, they realized that the job was going to be too big a project and too demanding on the customer. They quoted Slick Rick the outrageous price of $300,000 with fifty percent up front, and Slick decided to go somewhere else.

GOBLETS
(PIMP CUPS)

Originating in the underground pimp culture of Chicago, "pimp cups"—simple bar glasses transformed into ornate and elaborate fashion pieces—have firmly established their place in the world of bling. Seen worldwide in the movies, TV shows, and music videos of some of today's most influential purveyors of hip-hop culture—Snoop Dogg, Dave Chappelle, Bishop Don Juan, Lil Jon, and mainstream celebrities like Jimmy Kimmel, Jessica Simpson, and Tommy Lee, to name just a few—the pimp cup is the blingest of the bling.

On the Southside of Chicago lives the creator of the pimp cup phenomenon: Ms. Debbie the Glass Lady. Debbie isn't what you'd expect from the original Pimp Godmother, aka the official Pimp Cupstress. In her late forties, she's down to

THE PIMP CUPSTRESS

SNOOP AND DEBBIE
SHARE A WARM 'BLINGY' MOMENT.

earth and unassuming, sweet, and friendly. But like her pimp cups—part of the new bling/crunk movement blasting across the nation—Ms. Debbie is a true original. The craftsmanship, creativity, thoughtfulness, love, and spirituality that she brings to these cups are unquestionable.

When Debbie was a little girl, her mother would sometimes take her to the lamp factory where she worked as a designer. "She invented the pole lamp," Debbie recalls. "Even though she invented the lamp, she only earned about fifty cents an hour and never received credit for her invention." While Debbie's mother handcrafted and hand painted lamps, between thirty and forty per day, Debbie would sit on a desk and paint spare reject lamps. "I instantly fell in love with the colors," she says. After graduating from high school, in the early '70s, Debbie got a part-time position at the factory and started to create her own lamps. Meanwhile, her mother was painting things at home as gifts for the family—lamps, jelly jars, dishes, etc. As she began painting more glasses, she suggested to Debbie that they paint at Debbie's other job, bartending at some of Chicago's bars.

So Debbie painted a glass (the kind found in any Southside Chicago bar, any bar across the nation) for one of her favorite customers, Dennis Allen, ex-husband of Robin Robinson, one of the current anchors on Fox News in Chicago.

The cup didn't have any jewels, just a hand-painted design along with Allen's name in cursive. After she gave him the cup, a lot of her other customers approached her, asking, "Where's my glass?" She started painting more glasses at no charge and made it up in tips, which went through the roof. Soon she was selling the personalized glasses at various bars for about fifteen to twenty dollars a glass. Today if you go into any bar in the Southside of Chicago, you will find many of her old glasses.

Debbie's glasses continued to sell throughout the following decades. "I can't really explain why, but my glasses seem to make their owners very happy people. They make people smile," Debbie says. As her glasses became more and more popular, she started praying over each glass. "My mother once told me that if I prayed over all the money I received and

BISHOP DON "MAGIC" JUAN

prayed over every glass that I made, my business would always thrive. It was a way of giving back to God."

During the mid '90s, Debbie noticed that in hip-hop, a lot of rappers had begun to emulate, and rap about, the glamorous life. So she started to bling out her glasses by adding jewels. "Here they were, drinking expensive liquors, hanging out in exclusive bars, clubs, and hotels, with all this expensive jewelry and clothing, but they were drinking out of these cheap plastic cups! I was like, What's up with that?"

Debbie's first mainstream celebrity client was Bishop Don "Magic" Juan. Bishop had been purchasing some of her glasses from her "so-called sales reps," and eventually called her personally, saying that he wanted to meet and buy glasses directly from her. The first time he came to her house, Debbie was sick with the flu, with a fever of 104 degrees. "I watched him drive up my block in his funny-looking car, the green Rolls-Royce. He was dressed all flamboyant with all this stuff draped around him, and the first thing he said was, 'I want to make you famous and rich.' Of course I didn't want to hear all that, since I knew pimps all my life (my father was a pimp—he's listed in the Pimping Hall of Fame), and I was definitely in no mood to hear that pimp talk." Bishop noticed that she wasn't in her best mood and asked what was the

DAVE CHAPPELLE
UPON RECEIVING HIS
PIMP CUP FROM DEBBIE,
DAVE ANNOUNCES "I'M
OFFICIAL, BITCH!"

matter. She told him she was sick and would he just pay for his glass and leave. At that point, he did something that Debbie, in a million years, would never have expected. He laid his hand on her shoulder and prayed for her. "He prayed for me! I was shocked."

Calmly, he told her that ever since he'd received his first glass of hers (about four years before they met), he would only drink out of her glasses. Then he told her about all the people he knew in the Hollywood, music, and sports circles and how he was going to make her famous. He asked her to put a cross on his glass with his emeralds, but she declined. "I didn't want to disrespect the Lord in any manner, and he was a pimp. And I won't make glasses with any blasphemous images, risqué, occult, or any gang signs, since I don't want anything negative associated with my glasses."

Once Bishop ordered glasses for Mike Tyson (with boxing

PIMPSY
ONE OF DEBBIE'S BEST CUSTOMERS

gloves painted on them) and Pamela Anderson Lee, a lot of celebrities began to take notice. But after Bishop gave a glass to Snoop Dogg, that's when Debbie's business jumped to the next level. Snoop and her glasses became inseparable. Everywhere he appeared, he was prominently featured with one: from Jay Leno, to *The View*, to many of his films, Snoop always has a glass in his hand. "The funny thing is that my glasses weren't known as pimp cups until Snoop Dogg came along. In one of his videos he said something to the effect of 'Hand me my pimp cup.' Snoop officially named my glass the pimp cup."

Since then, Debbie's celebrity clientèle has only grown, to include Lil Jon (a die-hard fan who featured a glass on an album cover), Fat Joe, Roy Jones, Wendy Williams, Nelly, P. Diddy, 50 Cent, Lil' Flip, Juvenile, Outkast, Jalen Rose, Tom Joyner, Dave Chappelle, Halle Berry, and Paris Hilton.

"I've even pimped out beer mugs for members of Korn," says Debbie. As for people she'd like to make glasses for, at the top of the list are Madonna

DEBBIE'S PIMP CUPS START AT $300.

and Prince. "I view them as royalty, and they need to be drinking out of royal chalices." Other dream clients are Patti Labelle, Aretha Franklin, Jamie Foxx, and of course Bill Clinton, "for being an original, real Mack, and I know he would drink out of it. President Bush can't get my glass, because I think that would be a curse on my cups."

"My cups are special," Debbie says. "People go crazy over my cups because of the bling. It's all about the bling. Being able to see your name in lights."

five

BEHIND *the*

BLING

DIAMONDS ARE NOT AS RARE AS MANY PEOPLE THINK.
THEY ARE CERTAINLY NOT THE RAREST OF GEMSTONES;
THAT HONOR GOES TO RUBIES.

WE'VE ALL SEEN OUR FAVORITE CELEBRITIES ADORNED FROM HEAD TO TOE IN BLING. NOW THAT YOU'VE SEEN SOME OF THE ORIGINATORS, LET'S TAKE A BROADER LOOK AT SOME OF THE PLAYERS "BEHIND THE BLING."

A TWO-TIME ZONE WATCH FOR ALL YOU INTERNATIONAL PLAYERS

ARSHAD A. SALAM
Sailani Watches

From Sri Lanka, a country of beauty and serenity, come watches by Sailani, a company whose name fuses Eastern design and a Western context. Arshad A Salam, cofounder of Sailani (along with his brother Rashad and graphic designer Clyde Morgan Jr.), got his start in the jewelry business in Rochester, New York, in the late 1980s, polishing and soldering jewelry pieces. As his interest and experience grew, he began creating his own design ideas inspired by Arabic calligraphy. "Sri Lanka is world-renowned for its precious stones such as cat's-eyes, sapphires, and star rubies. Even the queen of England's crown is rumored to be adorned with stolen stones from Sri Lanka," quips Arshad. After working several years in Rochester, Arshad came to New York City and partnered with a designer. Together they operated a high-end jewelry boutique called Kamia (which means "blessed locket") that catered to models, celebrities, and Saudi royalty. It was there that Arshad started dabbling with colored diamonds: brown, pink, black, and purple, and diamonds with different cuts. He also began taking jewelry classes and apprenticed with a jeweler named Nissam Cohen. While working at Kamia, Arshad's brother was getting into the watch business. Rashad thought diamonds and watches made a good marriage and he consequently opened watch factories in China and in Hong Kong. "We see the future of watches and jewelry being very colorful," Arshad explained. "Colored stones in blinged-out watches. Sapphires, rubies, and garnets becoming more prevalent. Diamonds with different cuts, such as rose cuts, abstract designs, and transformer-style watches."

On the MP3 player screen:

Playlists
Groove Tunes >
Ultimate Dance Mix >
Romantic Songs >
Hip-Hop Classics >
Running Tracks >
On-The-Go >

On the pendant: MP3

On the watch: HKCE

**BLINGTIME
DOESN'T GET
BETTER
THAN THIS**
FUTURISTIC MP3 BLING
PIECES BY HKCE

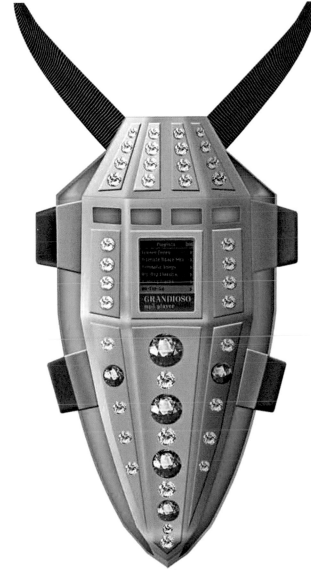

hat do Sean "P. Diddy" Combs, Jay-Z, Ja Rule, Justin Timberlake, Fred Durst, Mya, Busta Rhymes, Nelly, Usher, Pharrell, Wyclef Jean, Nas, Kelis, Tyrese, 50 Cent, Sharon and Ozzy Osbourne, Madonna, Jennifer Lopez, Bono, Michael Jordan, Tyson Beckford, Britney Spears, Sharon Stone, Beyoncé Knowles, Lenny Kravitz, Jessica Simpson, John Mayer—and the list goes on—all have in common? Unless you've been living under a rock for the past five-or-so years, you've probably heard of Jacob the Jeweler. Jacob & Co. was founded in 1981 by Jacob Arabo in New York City. Jacob Arabo's passion for jewelry began when he was a young boy in Russia. Just after immigrating to the United States with his family, he enrolled in jewelry design school, hoping to develop his natural talents; he quickly rose to the top of the class. Jacob opened a small booth in New York City's bustling diamond district and quickly began designing for a number of jewelry brands and private clients.

In the mid-1990s, R&B singer Faith Evans stumbled upon Jacob's place while shopping for jewelry for her upcoming CD cover. Completely taken by Jacob's creations, she quickly returned with her husband, the late Notorious B.I.G. The couple became loyal customers and recommended Jacob to a host of their high-profile friends, creating great interest throughout the music industry. The result was that Jacob & Co. became the place to go for custom jewelry, and Arabo was given the name "Jacob the Jeweler." Arabo has designed pieces for some of the most royal of hip-hop's royalty, and his venture as a watch designer and manufacturer (Jacob & Co. Watches) has taken off like a rocket.

JACOB
ARABO
REIGNING KING OF
BLING

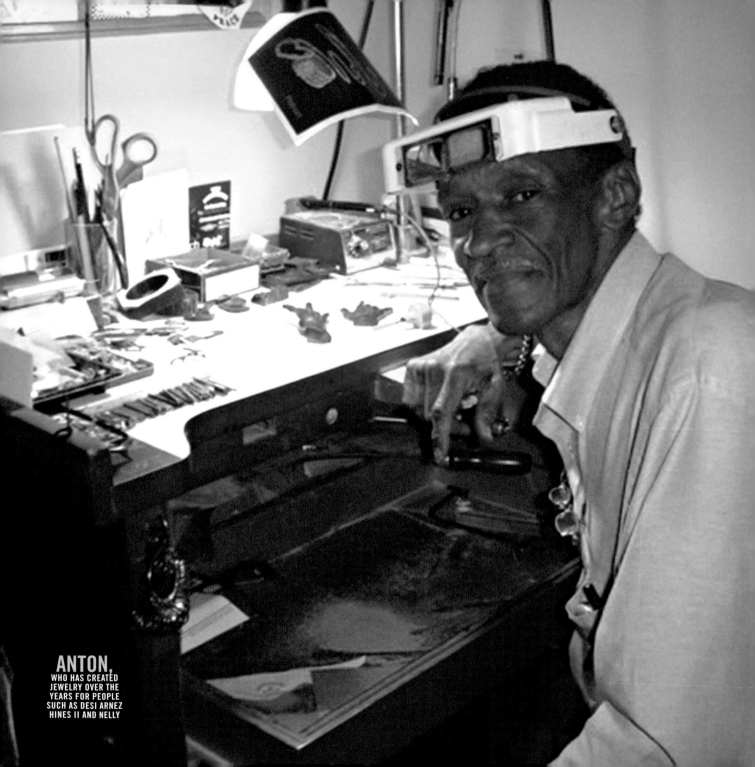

ANTON,
WHO HAS CREATED
JEWELRY OVER THE
YEARS FOR PEOPLE
SUCH AS DESI ARNEZ
HINES II AND NELLY

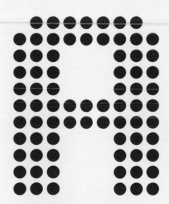

nton the Jeweler is a rare breed, a man who learned his craft by making iron lungs. In the late 1950s, an opportunity arranged by his father to meet a jeweler landed Anton a job as an apprentice at a jewelry company in New York City's diamond district, where he switched from working with steel and aluminum to manipulating gold and platinum. His first project was making platinum infinity rings—wedding bands with diamonds encrusted around the band. In those days, a jeweler was required to know almost every aspect of the jewelry-making process. After learning how to monogram, Anton began working at the exclusive David Webb jewelers. "The shop was segregated between Italians, Germans, Spaniards, Argentineans, and Cubans," Anton recalls. "Around sixty jewelers worked in the building, and I was the only black. I was fortunate because few jewelers hired blacks during this period." In 1968, Anton decided to open his own booth in a shop on 47th Street. It was on street level, and famous folks like Reverend Ike, singer Lou Rawls, Harlem gangster Nicky Barnes, Muhammad Ali, and a lot of the "Superfly" pimps (afghan dogs, bell bottoms, and big hats) used to come to Anton's booth. Though it was a great experience, after a while Anton closed his shop and started hustling his craft on

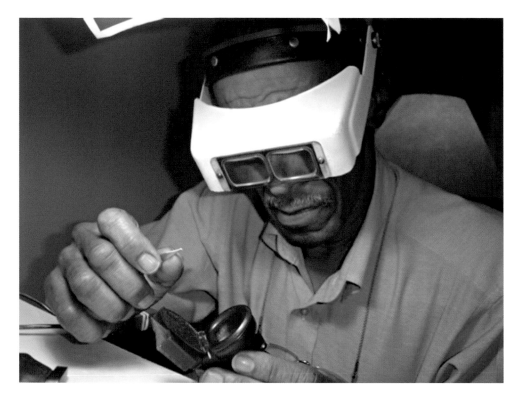

the street: He wasn't getting along with his old partner. He traveled to Oklahoma and then to California, where he did jewelry work for such Hollywood stars as Desi Arnez Hines II, Charles Bronson, and Leo Carrillo (Pancho Gonzales on *The Cisco Kid*). Over time, Anton moved to more wax work, involving less machinery, and lighter and more mobile models. "Now that I sculpt original designs with wax, all my tools can fit in a briefcase," Anton reveals. "I can work in hotels . . . everywhere." Some of Anton's most memorable designs are Ludacris's skull, Busta Rhymes's spider, Treach's lock with princess-cut diamonds, and pendants for Outkast. He created a signature piece for Nelly and one for Rap-A-Lot Records, as well as Chingy's and E-40's microphone piece (originally designed for Missy Elliott). As for his vision for the future of bling: "I'd like to create an operation where all aspects of jewelry making, from design to the actual product, are being done. Model maker is my title: Give me a picture of anything and I'll do it. I love new challenges."

THE ILLUSION OF DIAMOND SCARCITY AND DIAMONDS' INSTANT ASSOCIATION WITH THE CONCEPTS OF ROMANCE
AND AFFLUENCE CAN BE TRACED BACK TO A SUCCESSFUL ADVERTISING CAMPAIGN MOUNTED BY DE BEERS AND
THE NEW YORK AD AGENCY OF N.W. AYER & SON IN SEPTEMBER 1938.

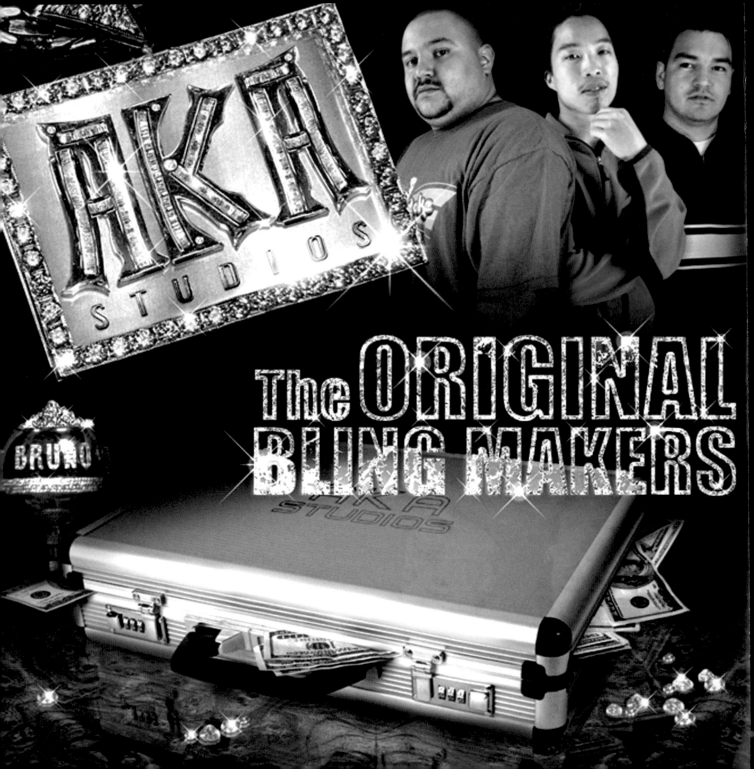

AKA STUDIOS

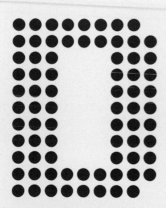

o you remember those blinged-out album covers during the mid- to late 1990s, the ones depicting rappers flaunting money, diamonds, cars, and sexy women, among other things, in some bugged-out visual hyperreality? These album covers and ads defined artists such as Master P, Eightball & MJG, Cash Money Millionaires, and countless indie-label rap artists from the Dirty South as well as the Midwest and the West Coast. Even Chris Rock paid homage to this visual iconography that personified bling with his *Bigger and Blacker* comedy album cover. If you wondered back in the day, while reading *The Source* or browsing in the hip-hop section at the record stores, "Who is making these works of art?" chances are it was Pen + Pixel Design. Run by brothers Aaron and Shawn Brock straight outta Houston, Texas, Pen + Pixel took album-cover art to the next level as its images depicted entire stories in one chaotic frame. Pen + Pixel no longer exists, but the dudes behind this often imitated but never duplicated style of artistic storytelling, Albert Mata and Adam Amaya, have regrouped and formed the new and improved AKA Studios. A few doors down from the shuttered Pen + Pixel office, at the same nondescript strip mall, these two talented graphic artists have designed over 7,000 bling-oriented album

CHRIS ROCK GETS HIS BLING ON.

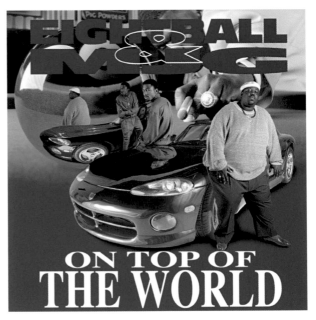

THE FIRST GROUP CREDITED FOR DISPLAYING
THE BLING LIFESTYLE LOOK, "MOMENTS" BEFORE MASTER P.

covers. According to Adam, the first artist to really "bling out" an album cover was Eightball & MJG. "We took pictures of them in a regular car and transformed it into something special. Eightball & MJG set the technique, the idea of bigger is better. Guys wanted to really differentiate themselves from each other and outdo themselves." As Adam recalls, it was Master P who took the look to the next level. "Our boss told P we would help him come out with some new album covers as we had just perfected the process of creating diamonds and color correcting. It took a lot of work perfecting that style... Working with diamonds graphically made us have to learn a new style of photography." There was a certain way Pen + Pixel's artwork was done, showing off the diamonds, gold, platinum, the cars close up, their grills, chrome wheels, etc. It was a perfect combination of photography and graphics.

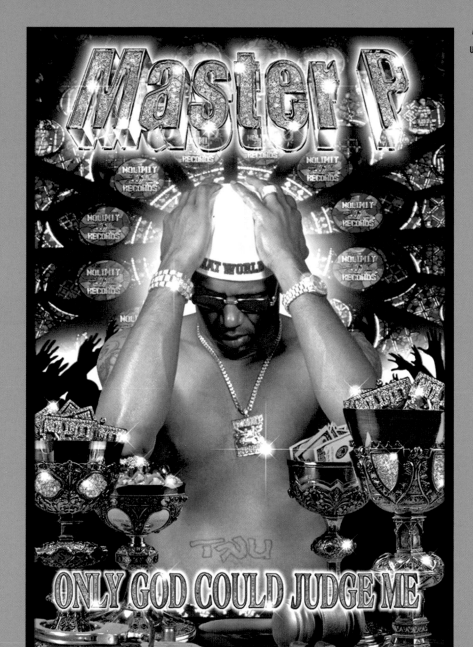

SILKK the SHOCKER

Charge It 2 Da Game

hat do Will Smith, Wyclef, Naomi Campbell, Brian "Baby" Williams, Jay-Z, and Allen Iverson all have in common? They have original signature pieces done by L.A.-based jeweler to the stars, Chris Aire, aka the Iceman. Aire's career in jewelry started after his graduation from Cal State University at Long Beach, where he was a film major. A friend's father knew of Chris's lifelong interest in gems and invited him to work with him. After six years of learning the ropes, Chris set off on his own; in 1996, 2Awesome International was born. Chris's first clients were NBA basketball players and celebrities like comedian Bill Bellamy. Chris, a certified gemologist, created and patented the hottest trend in jewelry, red gold, and his customized dog tags are some of the most popular among celebrities. In addition, the Iceman owns his own jewelry-manufacturing facility. Some of the Iceman's signature pieces are his limited edition Swiss-made Aire Traveler watches, which come in red gold, platinum, and steel, with or without diamonds. While these are the most-requested by celebrities and entertainers, his biggest seller is his red gold jewelry. Created by adding compatible red alloys to yellow gold, red gold is the most expensive gold. It sells for at a fraction of the cost of platinum, however, and has many of the same qualities, such as being hypoallergenic and nonirritating. As for the importance of bling, Chris says, "Bling means to me your ability to express yourself in a unique way, and that includes adorning yourself with expensive things like diamonds, cars, clothes, and shoes." The Iceman has spoken.

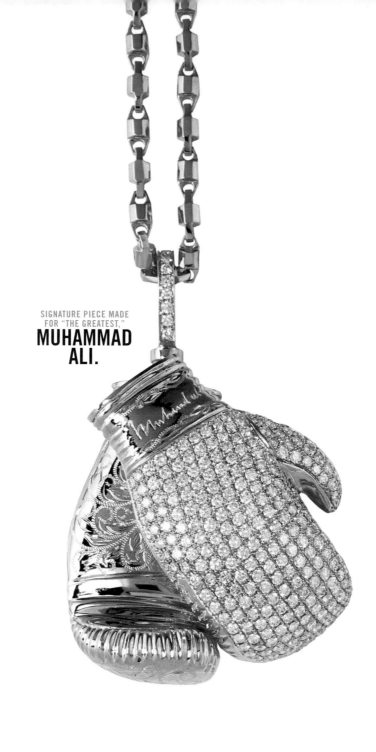

SIGNATURE PIECE MADE
FOR "THE GREATEST,"
**MUHAMMAD
ALI.**

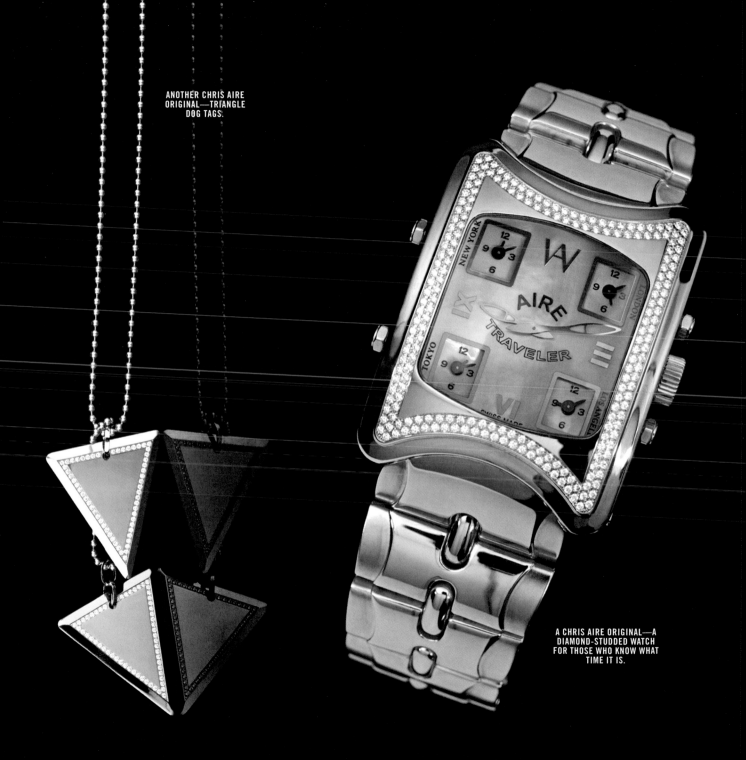

ANOTHER CHRIS AIRE
ORIGINAL—TRIANGLE
DOG TAGS.

A CHRIS AIRE ORIGINAL—A
DIAMOND-STUDDED WATCH
FOR THOSE WHO KNOW WHAT
TIME IT IS.

KEL 1st

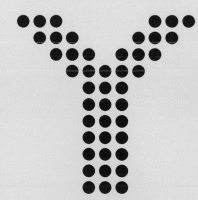

ou may not know him, but you've known his work for a long time. Former graffiti artist Kel 1st has had many careers, but the one that keeps calling him back is jewelry. "It all started with bombing transit back in the day—that was the key. I started painting on metal [the trains], and I eventually wanted to work in a three-dimensional medium." Kel 1st's first jewelry public appearance was way back in 1983 in the pilot episode (the only episode) of the seminal hip-hop TV classic *Graffiti Rock*. His girlfriend at the time, Debbie Mazar, was a background dancer. "I designed my very first nameplate pendant for her, and the next thing I knew, she was rocking my piece on television." Filmmaker, trendsetter, and resident avant-gardist Vincent Gallo (who appeared on *Graffiti Rock* as Prince Vince) also rocked one of Kel's nameplate medallions on that show. Kel was about to strike gold as Debbie hung out with a then unknown singer who went by the name of . . . Madonna (yes, *the* Madonna!). "Madonna dug Debbie's piece so much she

THE PIECE THAT STARTED IT ALL. MADE FOR ACTRESS DEBI MAZAR.

requested that I design her world-famous Boy Toy name buckle, as well as a lucky star pendant that she wore during her historical appearance on the 1984 MTV awards show," says Kel. Shortly after that, Kel 1st ventured into fashion, where he worked with some of the bigger houses, veering off the path of jewelry until about two years ago. Once again, a lucky girlfriend was able to receive an original Kel 1st piece, and once again, at a party, her girls rushed her to find out where she'd copped it. "Overnight, I was in the jewelry business again. My girl's piece had so many people requesting my work that I had to open up shop." From there, Kel 1st designed the ill Busta Rhymes belt buckle, Kelis's nameplate—featured in her "Milkshake" video—and an incredible Egyptian eyepiece for Afrika Bambaataa. The list of artists Kel 1st would like to work with in the future includes trendsetters like Missy Elliot, DJ Kayslay, 50 Cent, and the current reigning king of bling, Ghostface Killah.

BELT BUCKLE DESIGNED
FOR BUSTA RHYMES.

THE KING OF PLATINUM JEWELERS

n 125th Street, in the heart of Harlem, is the King of Platinum Jewelers. Run by Mike, a gemologist who opened the shop five years ago, who's assisted by two huge brothers aptly named Big Al (the in-house jewelry modeler) and Big Mike (security), this tiny shop has come to be the place to go in Harlem when it is time to get freshly dipped.

The three came together by chance. An artist his entire life, Big Al studied design at Rensselaer Polytechnic Institute; one day about two years ago, he came into the shop to buy some jewelry, and, the next thing he knew, he was working there as a modeler. A similar story is shared by Big Mike, a former law officer who has worked at the King of Platinum for the past four years after wandering in one afternoon to check out the bling.

"Here in Harlem, it's a true community," Mike says, explaining one of the main differences between 125th street and the diamond district. While the clientèle of this carefully priced jeweler is primarily local, there are plenty of celebrity clients who have come to the King of Platinum, including old-school legends like Melle Mel, Grandmaster Caz, and Pee Wee Dance of Zulu Nation fame. "About a year ago, we hooked up with LL Cool J," recalls Mike. "Once LL became a customer (and he's a great guy as well), our celebrity clientèle broke wide open." Now, the King of Platinum gets quite a few customers

DIAMOND IS THE HARDEST SUBSTANCE ON EARTH.

from the south, like T.I., as well as celebrities like Allen Iverson, Fat Joe, the Terror Squad, and Busta Rhymes.

LL Cool J's stylist invited the guys to his "Hush" video shoot, where they provided him with about a hundred thousand dollars' worth of jewelry. This led to more opportunities to provide styling services for artists who need bling for special events, videos shoots, and performances.

The King of Platinum's specialty? It is, without doubt, the pendant. There is an impressive display of pendants, pieces of every size, color, and shape, as well as customer-requested favorites, like the cartoon character Pinky from *Pinky and the Brain*.

"Jewelry has no race, and what I mean by that is that here, other than all the love and respect you get, you get great jewelry. It's not about race. It's not about nationality or religious background. It's all about the jewelry."

athmatiks, a design studio in Long Island City, New York, is responsible for an unforgettable piece of bling (that you may have been lucky enough to spot on a postcard): an intricate and detailed DJ turntable ring. The tiny needle arm rests on a diamond-encrusted table that actually spins. Maybe the most amazing thing about it is that it was their first project.

Dave and Hozi are the designers and owners of Mathmatiks. Dave grew up in Washington, D.C., lived in Thailand, and eventually moved to New York, where he enrolled as a student at the Fashion Institute of Technology. There he met his partner, Hozi, who was born in the Dominican Republic and grew up in the predominantly Hispanic Washington Heights, in New York City. When they met at FIT, Dave had already founded Mathmatiks, a design company based around the work of a small community of artistically inclined friends, a collective of individuals who knew it would be difficult to break their underground art into the mainstream's consciousness. Business grew steadily as various companies began to hire Mathmatiks to design logos and ads, and to style fashion shoots. Three years ago, Dave and Hozi moved to 145th and Broadway in New York City. Seeing the culture, how people lived and shopped, they decided it was time to design jewelry—and soon came up with their famous, ambitious DJ turntable ring.

"As designers, we always look to design anything; we're out here looking for the next challenge for our design skills. Our vision of jewelry has no ceiling," explains Hozi. "Everything we make we want to make based wholly on the vibe and look of our client."

Adds Dave, "Technology has really helped us in our creations. Because of the MP3, I can create jewelry that will play a bar of any song."

While they look forward to collaborating with established jewelers (like Cartier), Mathmatiks has dreams of designing for celebrities like Missy Elliot, 50 Cent, and Busta Rhymes—not to mention Snoop, for whom they already have a piece in mind. "It's a functional joint pendant, which can be used as a smoke pipe. The tip [the ash piece] of the joint is flooded with rocks that give you the impression that the joint is lit. The body of the piece is hollow, and the ash piece screws off so he can actually burn his stash."

AN ORIGINAL MATHMATIKS DJ RING CREATION CAN RUN ANY-WHERE FROM $15,000 TO $150,000, DEPENDING ON THE SIZE AND COMPLEXITY OF WHAT THE CLIENT DESIRES.

"We can make Jesus pieces with a light built in so that diamonds in his halo would be radiant!" Hozi exclaims. "Our mission is to incorporate technology in bling and see how far we can push the limits of jewelry."

appen

staying

dix

DIPPED

DIAMONDS ARE FOREVER.

BLING BIRTHSTONE CHART

- FEBRUARY: AMETHYST
- MARCH: AQUAMARINE
- APRIL: DIAMOND OR WHITE TOPAZ
- MAY: EMERALD
- JUNE: PEARL, ALEXANDRITE, OR MOONSTONE

- AUGUST: PERIDOT
- SEPTEMBER: SAPPHIRE
- OCTOBER: OPAL, PINK TOURMALINE
- NOVEMBER: TOPAZ
- DECEMBER: ZIRCON, TANZANITE, OR TURQUOISE

ZODIAC SIGN STONES

- ARIES (MARCH 22 TO APRIL 20): DIAMOND
- TAURUS (APRIL 21 TO MAY 21): EMERALD
- GEMINI (MAY 22 TO JUNE 21): AGATE
- CANCER (JUNE 22 TO JULY 22): PEARL OR MOONSTONE

- VIRGO (AUGUST 23 TO SEPTEMBER 22): SAPPHIRE
- LIBRA (SEPTEMBER 23 TO OCTOBER 23): OPAL
- SCORPIO (OCTOBER 24 TO NOVEMBER 21): SARDONYX
- SAGITTARIUS (NOVEMBER 22 TO DECEMBER 21): TOPAZ
- CAPRICORN (DECEMBER 22 TO JANUARY 21): ONYX
- AQUARIUS (JANUARY 21 TO FEBRUARY 21): TURQUOISE
- PISCES (FEBRUARY 22 TO MARCH 21): MOONSTONE

ANNIVERSARY STONES (AND SOME METALS)

* 1st: GOLD
* 2nd: GARNET
* 3rd: PEARL
* 4th: BLUE TOPAZ
* 5th: SAPPHIRE
* 6th: AMETHYST
* 7th: ONYX
* 8th: TOURMALINE
* 9th: LAPIS LAZULI
* 10th: DIAMOND
* 11th: TURQUOISE
* 12th: JADE
* 13th: CITRINE
* 14th: OPAL
* 15th: RUBY
* 20th: EMERALD
* 25th: SILVER
* 30th: PEARL
* 35th: EMERALD
* 40th: RUBY
* 45th: SAPPHIRE
* 50th: GOLD
* 55th: ALEXANDRITE
* 60th: DIAMOND

STAYING DIPPED! Directory

Holla at these folks we've featured if you are looking to get your bling on for yourself—or purchase it for that someone special.

ABC JEWELERS
Anton the Modeler
678-508-3493
www.abcjewelers.com

AKA STUDIOS
2400 Central Parkway
Suite J
Houston, TX 77092
Tel: 713-680-3554
Fax: 713-680-0563
Email: aka@akastudios.com
www.akastudios.com

2AWESOME INTERNATIONAL
P.O. Box 811726
Los Angeles, CA 90081
877-500-AIRE #(2743)
Tel: 213-688-0900
Fax: 213-688-2880
http://2awesomeint.com/index.htm
info@chrisaire.com

AVIANNE & CO., INC.
28 West 47th Street
New York, NY 10036
212-768-3360

THE HOUSE OF BIJAN
420 North Rodeo Drive
Beverly Hills, CA 90210
310-273-6544
www.bijan.com

DEBBIE THE GLASS LADY
773-783-0825
www.debbietheglasslady.com

EDDIE'S FAMOUS GOLD TEETH
2925 Headland Drive
Greenbriar, GA
404-349-2533, 404-438-1758
and
82 Peachtree Street
Downtown at the Underground
404-222-9017
www.eddiesgoldtooth.com

HONG KONG CENTRAL
ENTERPRISE LTD.
Level 25, Bank of China Tower,
1 Garden Road, Central, Hong Kong
Tel: 852-2251-8652
Fax: 852-2251-1618

JACOB & CO.
48 West 57th Street,
Fourth Floor
New York, NY 10022
866-522-6210
contact@jacobandco.com
www.jacobandco.com

KING OF PLATINUM JEWELRY
236 West 125th Street
New York, NY 10027
212-663-9737

KEL 1ST JEWELS
917-296-6590
info@kel1st.com
www.kel1st.com

MANNY'S OF NEW YORK
Tito
71 West 47th Street
Booth 11
New York, NY 10036
(212) 764-1089
madjwlr@aol.com
www.mannysofnewyork.com

MATHMATIKS
Lifestyle Design Studio
40–17 22nd Street,
Fifth Floor
Long Island City, NY 11101
646-472-5849
www.mathmatiks.com

DR. MARK JACKSON
DR. RONALD CUNNING
Precision Ceramics
Dental Laboratory
9591 Central Avenue
Montclair, CA 91763
800-223-6322
mjackson@pcdl-usa.com
http://hiphopdentistry.com
www.pcdl-usa.com

SETS | sale! SINGLE PLATES | sale! DOUBLE PLATES | sa

Bling Care and Maintenance Tips

Just bought a new timepiece? A blinged-out tennis bracelet or a pimped-out pinky ring? The Gemological Institute of America—the world's foremost authority in gemology—offers the following tips on diamond care.

➤ **HANDLE YOUR DIAMOND SPARINGLY.** Because diamonds are natural magnets for grease, they're not easy to keep clean. Handling a diamond with your fingers provides enough oil from your skin (the type of "grease" that most affects diamonds) to alter the way your diamond looks.

➤ **CLEAN YOUR DIAMOND REGULARLY.** A simple plan to keep your diamond jewelry always looking beautiful is to soak the diamond in an ammonia-based household cleaner (such as window cleaner) overnight, once or twice weekly. In the morning, remove the diamond from the cleaner and brush it with a soft, clean toothbrush (one that has not previously been used in any way and that you reserve exclusively for cleaning your diamond) to remove any leftover dirt. Take extra care to brush the back of the diamond, as this will be the area that has collected the most oil and dirt.

➤ **BE AWARE THAT FRAGILE SETTINGS WON'T TAKE KINDLY TO BEING SCRUBBED WITH A TOOTHBRUSH, SO USE A SOFT TOUCH.** Then, just rinse the diamond with water and wipe with a soft, lint-free cloth.

➤ **DON'T USE HARMFUL SOLUTIONS.** Chlorine (as in household bleach) and abrasives (such as household cleansers and toothpaste) should never be used when cleaning diamonds, especially those set in jewelry. These erode some of the metals often used in diamond settings and may loosen prongs, or even dissolve the metal completely.

➤ **SOMETIMES AN ULTRASONIC CLEANER IS NECESSARY** to remove encrusted dirt from diamonds. By sending high-frequency sound waves through a detergent solution, ultrasonic cleaners cause vibrating fluid to remove accumulated dirt and grime. They can also shake loose stones from their mounting, however, so this method shouldn't be used on fragile settings and is best undertaken by a professional jeweler.

➤ **REGULAR CLEANING** will keep your diamond jewelry in gleaming condition and ready to sparkle on that special occasion.

➤ **IF YOU HAVE QUESTIONS ON DIAMOND CARE,** seek the advice of a qualified jeweler—ideally someone educated at the Gemological Institute of America. Visit the Institute's Web site at www.gia.edu.

➤ **FOR FINE WATCHES,** you should occasionally remove the timepiece from its band and brush in hard-to-reach areas using a very soft toothbrush.

➤ **IF YOU BUY GOLD FRONTS,** Eddie and the hip-hop dentists agree that you should brush your teeth and fronts regularly with gel-type toothpaste and a soft-bristle toothbrush. Get periodic polishing of your fronts, and don't forget to floss!

Some Things to Know When Shopping for Your Diamonds*

The 5 Cs of diamonds: carat, cut, color, clarity, and cost.

CARAT: A unit of weight for precious stones, equivalent to 200 milligrams. Number of carats indicates only weight; carats have nothing to do with size. The heavier (in mass) the diamond, the more carats it's got.

CUT: The cut of a diamond can affect its price significantly. Cut refers to the exact size and proportions of a finished diamond. How a diamond is cut determines the sparkle, or brilliance, of the stone. A well-cut stone allows light to enter and refract through the facets, which creates brilliance. A stone that is too shallow or too deep will have limited brilliance, resulting in a dull and lifeless look. Various cuts include brilliant, radiant, and emerald.

COLOR: Though most diamonds appear colorless to the untrained eye, they do have subtle shade differences. The diamond industry uses a range of letters to grade color, from D (colorless) to Z (light yellow). A diamond with less color or intense color is more valuable, and therefore, more expensive.

CLARITY: This is the clearness of appearance when you look into a diamond. The clarity scale ranges from flawless to imperfect. A flawless diamond will cost more than a similar diamond with flaws. The natural imperfections in diamonds are called inclusions and consist of minerals or crystals trapped inside the stone during its formation. The number and distinctiveness of the inclusions determine the clarity of the diamond. Diamonds that have no inclusions will reflect more light and are extremely rare. Nearly all diamonds contain these inclusions; they contribute to each stone's uniqueness. Most inclusions are invisible to the untrained eye: A jeweler's loupe is necessary to detect them.

COST: The first four Cs (carat, cut, color, and clarity) determine the price a diamond will command.

*Source: Gemological Institute of America and European Gemological Laboratory (U.S.)

Diamond Color Chart

D	E	F	G	H	I	J	K	L	M	N	O	P	Q	R	S	T	U	V	X	Y	Z
COLORLESS			NEARLY COLORLESS				FAINT YELLOW			VERY SLIGHT YELLOW				LIGHT YELLOW							

How to Buy Diamonds That Are Conflict- or Blood-Free

Ask your jeweler whether he or she buys from trusted suppliers who guarantee conflict-free warranties on their stones.

Consider purchasing Canadian diamonds, which have a certificate all the way from the mine to the store, unlike diamonds supplied through the Kimberley Process*, a system that claims to track the export of ninety-eight percent of the world's rough diamonds from the mine only to their entry into another participating country.

*The Kimberley Process is a joint government, international diamond industry, and civil society initiative to stem the flow of conflict diamonds, rough diamonds used by rebel movements to finance wars against legitimate governments. The trade in these illicit stones has contributed to devastating conflicts in countries such as Angola, the Democratic Republic of Congo, and Sierra Leone. The Kimberley Process Certification Scheme is an innovative, voluntary system that imposes extensive requirements on participants to certify that shipments of rough diamonds are free of conflict diamonds. The Kimberley Process is composed of forty-three participants, including the European Community. For more information: www.kimberleyprocess.com.

Consider buying diamonds created artificially, or "above ground," by companies such as Gemesis (www.gemesis.com) and Apollo Diamond (www.apollodiamond.com), two companies leading the way in manufacturing "cultured diamonds" that are indistinguishable from mined ones and are sold at a fraction of the cost. These diamonds have been reported to seem so like mined ones, that only high-end diamond-grading equipment can detect the difference. Last, don't sleep on cubic zirconia. With recent advances in technology, cubic zirconia is starting to hold its own. Check out Diamond Essence (www.diamondessence.com), a leading designer and marketer of the high-quality 14-karat gold cubic zirconia and other simulated-gem jewelry. At the end of the day, who's gonna know the difference? Just you and your jeweler.

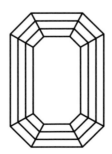

If You Can't Afford to Buy Any Diamonds, Make Your Own

A Complete Procedure to Produce Diamonds: Low-Energy Nuclear Transmutation / Alchemy aka Fresh Diamonds Made in the Microwave

A RECIPE BY JOE CHAMPION, WWW.RANGEGUIDE.NET

The authors and publishers of this book do not vouch for the authenticity of this recipe and should not be held liable for any kitchen mess you make. Do not attempt this experiment without competent adult supervision!

➤ **STEP 1** Using a Pyrex microwave cooking dish with lid, place two charcoal briquettes covered with 4 ounces of peanut butter inside. Microwave on high for 60 minutes at 10-minute intervals.

➤ **STEP 2** When cool enough to handle, take the dish outdoors and place on top of an unlit barbeque grill. Remove the lid from the dish and saturate the charcoal and residue with charcoal lighter fluid. Light the charcoal. (Note: At this time the diamonds are made, this procedure is reducing the excess carbon to ash.)

➤ **STEP 3** At this time you should have a dish full of gray/black soot. Carefully scrape this soot into a dark colored dish and gently wash. The ash will wash away leaving the diamonds you've produced.

If you decide to experiment with recipes other than the one above, do so with competent adult supervision and in extremely well-ventilated areas or outdoors. Joe Champion has released the recipe above due to its safety and lack of possible toxicity in your kitchen.

NINE FAMOUS DIAMONDS THAT WOULD MAKE YOU THE REAL KING OF BLING

1. THE CENTENARY
2. THE EUREKA
3. THE HORTENSIA
4. THE JUBILEE
5. THE KOH-I-NOOR
6. THE NIARCHOS
7. THE SANCY
8. THE TIFFANY
9. THE MILLENNIUM STAR*

* Weighing in at 777 carats, this De Beers-owned rock is considered priceless. The Millennium Star was discovered by some villagers in the Democratic Republic of the Congo, in Africa. Because the villagers didn't have a bank account, De Beers paid cash for it (many millions; according to De Beers), and the villagers buried the money in the ground, where it was partially eaten by insects. The money has since been dug up and deposited in a foreign bank account for safekeeping.

Shout-outs to www.finejewelrydesigns.com, www.robbinsdiamonds.com, www.diamondgrading.com.

TOP TEN BLING HEIST FILMS

1) *TOPKAPI* (1964)
2) *THE PINK PANTHER* (1964)
3) *GOLDFINGER* (1964)
4) *KELLY'S HEROES* (1970)
5) *DIAMONDS ARE FOREVER* (1971)
6) *THE HOT ROCK* (1972)
7) *A FISH CALLED WANDA* (1988)
8) *RESERVOIR DOGS* (1992)
9) *THREE KINGS* (1999)
10) *HEIST* (2001)
BONUS: *AFTER THE SUNSET* (2004)

5 BLINGED-OUT MOVIE CHARACTERS

CASTOR TROY, *FACE OFF* (blinged-out .45 automatic pistols). • AURIC GOLDFINGER, *GOLDFINGER* (in gold from head to toe). • MR. BIG, *I'M GONNA GET YOU SUCKA!* (died from being an O.G. (Over-Golded). • JIMMY JUMP, *KING OF NEW YORK* (Larry Fishburne kept it old school with the four finger rings, gold teeth, and dookie ropes). • CLEOPATRA, *CLEOPATRA* (Elizabeth Taylor, one of the original queens of bling). • BONUS: ZHAO, James Bond's *DIE ANOTHER DAY* (Zhao had diamonds embedded in one side of his face. Now that's gangsta!

OUR BLING MIXTAPE MASHUP—THE B SIDES

1) "DIAMONDS ARE FOREVER" (JAY-Z)
2) "DIAMONDS FROM SIERRA LEONE" (KANYE WEST)*
3) "CONFLICT DIAMONDS" (LUPE FIASCO)*
4) "GOLDDIGGER" (EPMD)
5) "PAID IN FULL" (ERIC B & RAKIM)
6) "LOOKING AT MY GUCCI" (SCHOOLLY D)
7) "FAT GOLD CHAIN" (SCHOOLLY D)
8) "LUCY IN THE SKY WITH DIAMONDS" (THE BEATLES)
9) "BLING, BLING" (B.G. of CASH MONEY MILLIONAIRES)
10. "DIAMONDS IN MY PINKY RING" (LIL' SCRAPPY)
 BONUS: "DIAMONDS" (LIL JON & EAST SIDE BOYZ)

* There seems to be some disagreement as to which song is original as both sample Shirley Bassey's "Diamonds Are Forever." Many claim that Lupe's version was released earlier than Kanye's version.

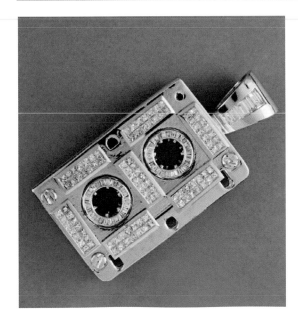

MOST BLINGED OUT-TV SHOWS

MTV CRIBS
HOW I'M LIVIN', BET
MIAMI VICE, NBC
THE GOTTIS, A&E
THE FABULOUS LIFE OF . . . , VH1

FIVE WORST PLACES TO GO WITH YOUR BLING ON

1 THE NEW YORK CITY SUBWAY
2 THE CORNER OF FLORENCE AND NORMANDY, LOS ANGELES
3 RODEO DRIVE, BEVERLY HILLS
4 SOUTHEAST WASHINGTON, D.C.
5 NEW LOTS AVENUE, BROOKLYN
6 BONUS: HOT 97 RADIO STATION, NEW YORK CITY

MOST ILLEST BLING IN HIP-HOP

* Black Rob's medallion modeled after his own face by Avianne & Co., New York City.
* The Queensborough Bridge medallion made by Avianne & Co. with Nas in mind but never bought by him. If interested in this piece, holla at Avianne & Co.
* The G-Unit Spinner medallion.
* Ghostface Killah's Golden Eagle worn on his arm.
* Ludacris's "human medallion" in his "Stand Up" video.

MOST BLINGED-OUT HISTORICAL FIGURES

* KING TUT
* MONTEZUMA
* QUEEN ELIZABETH II
* THE HOUSE OF SAUD
* THE QUEEN OF SHEBA
* QUEEN NEFERTITI
* KING SOLOMON
* THE POPE
* SHAH JAHAN (THEN PRINCE KHURRAM) OF INDIA
* KING LOUIS XIV

FOUR PEOPLE WHO SHOULD LEAVE BLING ALONE

- ALI G, *THE ALI G SHOW*
- AARON CARTER, TEENAGE HEART-THROB SINGER
- BRIGITTE NIELSEN AND . . .
- FLAVOR FLAV, VH1'S *THE SURREAL LIFE*

WACKEST HIP-HOP BLING

- FAT JOE'S BACARDI BAT MEDALLION.
- TREACH FROM NAUGHTY BY NATURE'S PADLOCK AND CHAIN.
- DMX'S DOG-COLLAR HALTER TOP.
- ANYTHING WORN BY ALI G.

INFAMOUS BLING

- THE HOPE DIAMOND. Cursed everyone who had it.
- THE "ONE RING," *Lord of the Rings*. "Yessss, my precious . . . "
- THE ARK OF THE COVENANT. From the Bible.
- JA RULE'S CHAIN. The one 50 Cent allegedly snatched and put on his album *Guess Who's Back*.
- THE DEATH ROW PENDANT. Allegedly snatched by the late Crip Orlando Anderson, possibly leading to the "chain" of events that caused Tupac's demise.
- THE CROWN JEWELS OF ENGLAND. Ill-gotten jewels from England's various conquests back in the day.

BLINGED-OUT ATHLETES

- **ALLEN IVERSON**, basketball
- **DEION SANDERS**, football, basketball
- **SHAQUILLE O'NEAL**, basketball
- **WALT FRAZIER**, basketball
- **MIKE TYSON**, boxing
- **JOE NAMATH**, football
- **THE LEGENDARY PEE WEE KIRK-LAND**, New York City playground basketball
- **MICHAEL VICK**, football

TOP FIVE BLINGED-OUT RIDES
1. MAYBACH 2. BENTLEY
3. ROLLS-ROYCE 4. CADILLAC
5. MERCEDES-BENZ

FIVE CELEBRITIES WHO HAVE BEEN VICTIMS OF BLING THEFT

* JA RULE, in 1999. Was robbed of his chain, which resulted in the feud between Murder Inc. and G-Unit.
* TUPAC SHAKUR, in 1994. Was shot and robbed of $40,000 worth of jewelry outside a New York recording studio.
* STEPHON MARBURY, in 2000. Was robbed of a diamond necklace valued at $150,000 while sitting in his Bentley at a stoplight in New York.
* JACK OSBOURNE, in 2005. Had $382,000 worth of bling stolen from his suitcase on a flight from Los Angeles to London.
* NELLY, in 2003. Had more than $1 million worth of bling stolen from his hotel room in Las Vegas.
* HONORABLE MENTION: Rapper T.I., in 2005. Was relieved of an undisclosed amount of bling while exiting a New York nightclub. Rumor had it that the jewels turned up later at a Queens barbershop.

BLING ACCESSORIES WE'D LIKE TO SEE ON THESE FIVE HIP-HOP STARS

* MF DOOM: a black diamond-encrusted face mask.
* 50 CENT: a diamond-studded platinum bullet-proof vest.
* LIL' KIM: rose-gold-plated handcuffs.
* LUDACRIS: a gold-plated codpiece (shout-out to Larry Blackmon of Cameo).
* SNOOP DOGG: a gold-and-diamond-encrusted blunt medallion.

YOU KNOW YOU'RE CORNY WHEN YOU HAVE THE FOLLOWING ITEMS BLINGED OUT

* YOUR IPOD CASE.
* YOUR SNEAKERS.
* YOUR 2WAY.
* YOUR TOILET (SHOUT-OUT TO RUSSELL AND KIMORA LEE SIMMONS).
* YOUR CELL PHONE.
* YOUR SUNGLASSES.
* YOUR PANTIES.

YOU KNOW YOU'RE BLINGING WHEN...

1. JACOB THE JEWELER RETURNS YOUR CALLS.
2. YOUR FAMILY AND FRIENDS START SCHEMING ON YOU.
3. P. DIDDY ASKS TO BORROW YOUR BLING FOR HIS NEXT VIDEO.
4. YOUR BLING IS FEATURED ON *MTV CRIBS*, AND THE NEXT DAY THE IRS COMES TO AUDIT YOU (SHOUT-OUT TO JERMAINE DUPRI).
5. YOUR BLING IS WORTH MORE THAN THE GROSS NATIONAL PRODUCT OF SOME SMALL COUNTRY.

BLING BY ANY OTHER NAME:
1. ICE
2. ROCKS
3. SUGAR POPS
4. FROSTY FREEZE
5. BLOOD STONES
6. CANDY

COLOR GRADING SCALE BY G.I.A.

DEF	GHIJ	KLMN	OPQRSTU	VWXYZ
colorless	near colorless	faint yellow	very light yellow	fancy yellow

CLARITY GRADING SCALE

FL/IF	VVS-1	VVS-2	VS-1	VS-2	SI-1	SI-2	I-1	I-2	I-3

FI : Flawless
VVS : Very very slight inclusions
VS : Very slight inclusions
SI : Slight inclusions
I : Imperfect

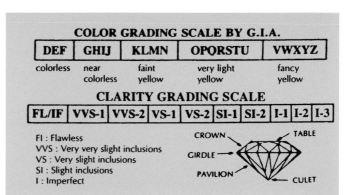

Acknowledgments

REGGIE: To my wife Akim and sons Chuma, Chi, and Kai Ossé, you guys are the true bling in my life. Beatrix Jean-Francois (mom), hopefully I've made you proud. Teddy Vann (the most amazing father-in-law a son in law could ask for). Gayle Grant—without you, we would never have conceived of the prospect of writing a book. Greg "Chyna" Cummins. Miyuki Mythril and the Mythril family. Brett Wright—(thank you, even though it didn't work out. Fritz Celestin—thanks for being a good friend and for providing fun times ever since 1977. Bob Celestin—thanks for getting that door open back in 1989. The entire Celestin family (thanks for the hold down). Super DJ/producer Clark Kent—you deserve the best. The Franklin family. The entire music industry—thanks for the experience and the memories. Ian Niles—thanks for holding me down during my harsh times and especially during yours. Wan Ling Dong Vann. The entire Vann family. Wan Chor Dong—whaddup yo? P. Diddy for the early music industry support, record shout-outs, and inspiration. Ian Waldon. Don Wade. Eric Sutton. Louise C. West, Esq. Roodolf and Jessica Senecal. Park Slope Bikram Yoga Studio, let's sweat it out! John Fleming at Chase Bank—thanks for not discriminating. Sharon Redman—thanks for looking out. Donna Walker-Kuhne for your continued guidance, support, and inspiration. Frank Forde. The Forde Family. Ron Lewis. Ken, P.J., and the entire Lincoln Place crew. Crown Heights. Downtown Brooklyn for the experience, the influence, and the inspiration. Angelo Ellerbee. Harve Pierre— thanks for the years, bro. The Jeannot family. Robert F. Kennedy Incentive Program. Xavier High School. Cornell University (Ujama, whadddup?). Georgetown University Law Center. Sam Galloway (Where the hell you at, bro? Some of this book is for you too!). Phi Beta Sigma, Kappa Xi Chapter—"Blue Phi!" Russell Simmons (Def Jam) and Andy Tavel, Esq. for giving me my very first music industry break. Bill Adler for the advice and access. Rachel Goldstein, Linda Goldstein, and the entire Goldstein family. The Bordes family. St. John's Place, Utica Avenue, Nostrand Avenue, Troy Avenue, all of Brooklyn, and all of New York City! Sharon Ingram, Aimee Camilien, and Maya, thanks for being great neighbors. Ms. Alice Atkinson. The Vick family. Derek Durham at Prospect Gardens Pharmacy—dude, what more can I say? Byron Crawford and Combat Jack at ByronCrawford.com. Chip Smith—Nam Myoho Renge Kyo. The Smith family. Arthur Young for your wisdom, support, and guidance. Michael and Barbara Walters. Soka Gakkai International, Daisaku Ikeda, Infinity District.

GABE: The Creator. The Tolliver family near and dear: Mom, Dad, Judy, Stephen, Merry, Chris, Dougie, Danny, Chanel, Jesse Bey, Darren, Lafe, John Tolliver, and the rest of the family—you know who you are. My cousin Robin Roberts—thank you for believing in me—much love always. Gail Huggins-Porter. Jud Laghi (ICM). Fiona Bloom, a true friend—much love. Sharon Pendana for your friendship, love, and support and for the Bijan discovery. Crystal Whaley. Paul "Orlo Fresh" Bixler. Kimson "Angola Red" Albert. Bryan "Truck Turner" & Florence & Max Adams. Jee Kim & Dominique Brown. Emir

"The Emirian" Lewis & family. Nick & Donna Charles and family. Jake Ann Jones & family. Debi & Josh Beckles. Vinay Chowdhry. Christina Booth. Ron Duncan. Gina Paige. Jay Lathon. Sandye Wilson. Garland "Buck Caesar" Farwell. Tanya Cuevas-Martinez. Fritz Celestine. Stan Lathan & Russell Simmons. Martha Diaz. Bryant Terry. Doug "Dub Asher" Carter. Ab & Priscilla. Beth & Carl. Kathleen Lott. Egotrip crew: Sacha, Chairman Mao, Gabe, Brent, & Elliot. Rachel Goldstein. Bill Adler. Sheril Antonio. Tamara Dreisinger. Andrea Benedict. Lauren Moore. Lisa Barnable. Kate & Ali Daniels. Todd, Nansi, Brandon & Lee Borum. Astrid Cooper. Mike Gallacchio. Andrea Westerman. Toni Dubois. Kenyatta Cheese. Tricia Wang. Natty Nat. Greg Fuller. Brian Cohen—haven't forgotten. Walter Mudu. Togo. Puma. If you feel you should be thanked or I forgot you, sign your name here: _____.

BLING JEWELERS, CREATORS, & CONTRIBUTORS:

Tito: Thank you for believing in the project and setting the record straight. Eddie Plein and family, Kevin, Jahvannie, Dezo, and Mr. Anton for your hospitality, gold teeth, and stories. Avi, Joey, Izzy, Arsen, and Gabriel of Avianne & Co. for blessing us. Chris Aire, Stacey, and Emily of 2awesome International. AKA studios: Adam Amaya, Hui-Kee Wong, and Albert Matas. Dr. Mark Jackson and Dr. Cunning of Precision Ceramics Dental Laboratory. The House of Bijan: Mr. Bijan & Jayne Brandonisio. Debbie the Glass Lady & Carlin Tools for the Chicago hospitality and letting us tell your story. Hong Kong Central Enterprises: Arshad and Rashad Abdul Salam & Ed Lovelace. Urbandictionary.com, Fred Cuellar aka The Diamond Guy, Julie Seitz, Diamond Cutters International, Radhika Sarin, earthworksaction.org, nodirtygold.org, The Liberace Foundation, Kel 1st—the future, Dave and Hozi—Mathamatiks, Mike, Big Mike, and Big Al—Kings of Platinum, 125th Street—Uptown representing!—Roxy, and lastly, Jacob the Jeweler.

PHOTOGRAPHERS WITHOUT WHOM THIS BOOK WOULDN'T BE POSSIBLE:

Ernie "Where's My Check" Paniccioli, much appreciation and love for the photos. Atsuko Tanaka for your dope photos. Jeanette Beckman, London Features International, Getty Photo Archives, RETNA, John Ricard, Corbis, Al Pereira, Sue Kwon, Photofest, Robert Burch, David Corio.

GOT QUESTIONS, BLING, OR BEEF? blingjewelrybook@yahoo.com

PHOTO CREDITS